VALUES IN CONFLICT

VALUES IN CONFLICT

32nd COUCHICHING CONFERENCE, C.I.P.A.

Edited by T. E. H. Reid

Published for Canadian Institute on Public Affairs
by University of Toronto Press

The Canadian Institute on Public Affairs, 244 St. George St., Toronto, Ontario, Canada, is a private non-profit organization which aims to bring together at its two annual conferences people of diverse beliefs and backgrounds, with a view to promoting mutual understanding and clearer insight about issues of major public concern. No attempt is made to reach decisions or pass resolutions. The Institute, as such, is precluded from expressing an opinion on any aspect of public affairs. Opinions expressed in this publication by Conference speakers are not, therefore, those of the Institute.

© University of Toronto Press, 1963
Library of Congress Catalogue Card Number: 63-22478
Printed in Canada
Reprinted in 2018
ISBN 978-1-4875-7310-2 (paper)

PREFACE

The views expressed in this book focus on man's values in Western civilization today. The authors explore the development of our values and examine their foundations in the attempt to see if they are based on concepts which are valid for contemporary society. Some of the authors conclude that a core of values exists universally, immutable through time. Others take a contrary view—that man's values are created and destroyed by the continuous revolutions in his knowledge of himself and of his environment.

Of central concern is the question of *conflict*. Do our espoused values contradict one another? Are we hypocritical in the day-to-day application of our values in our personal, family, religious, and social life, in politics, and in our economic activities? And, if so, to what extent?

The ten authors come from a variety of backgrounds. They were carefully selected in order to represent a wide spectrum of political, economic, and religious viewpoints. In addition, they approach *values in conflict* from different disciplines: sociology, political science, psychology, history, philosophy, economics, theology, and aesthetics. Often their views on our values meet in the depths of their individual disciplines with startling clarity.

The articles need not be read in order. Each is self-contained. Some indication of the approach taken and the sphere discussed is given by the short titles.

The book includes a selected bibliography prepared for those readers who wish to know more about various aspects of the values of Western societies. It is divided into seven sections: general, social, philosophy and religion, personal, science, politics, and economics. Books and articles by the contributors to this volume are included.

The articles are written by the speakers of the 32nd Couchiching Conference. The Conference was presented by the Canadian Institute on Public Affairs in co-operation with the Canadian Broadcasting Corporation at Geneva Park, Ontario, July 27–31, 1963, under the chairmanship of Mr. Ronald S. Ritchie. Like the Winter Conference (held each year since 1955) it is open to members of the Institute and the public, and brings together approximately two hundred persons from many walks of life including business, labour, government, universities, and the press.

Plenary sessions were held on four evenings and three mornings. Less than half of each two-hour session was devoted to formal addresses by the speakers since the tradition of Couchiching is to place the major emphasis on questions and comments from the floor by the resident participants.

Small informal discussion groups met throughout and formed a vital part of the conference. The speakers also participated in the discussion groups, which, unlike the plenary sessions, were held "off the record." The group meetings were most lively and a great deal of credit is due to their Convenor, Mr. Edward D. Greathed, and to the nine leaders: Clayton Baxter, Professor of Philosophy, Mount Allison University; Pierre de Bellefeuille, Editor, *Le Magazine Maclean*; Arnold Edinborough, Editor, *Saturday Night Publications*; William Kilbourn, Chairman, Humanities Division, York University; Paul Lacoste, Professeur de Philosophie, Université de Montréal; William Nicholls, Professor of Religious Studies, University of British Columbia; Ronald St. J. Macdonald, Professor of Law, University of Toronto; Charles Taylor, Professor of Political Science, McGill University; Vincent Tovell, Television Producer, Canadian Broadcasting Corporation.

The first hour of each plenary session was carried on the Trans-Canada radio network of the Canadian Broadcasting Corporation. The CBC also featured the speakers on a special one-hour television programme on the last day of the conference which highlighted the controversial points of view expressed during the previous four days.

The Institute wishes to thank all the speakers, chairmen, and group leaders who devoted their thoughts, time, and energy to the other participants in the Conference. The Institute is grateful to the office staff, the six student scholars, the Librarian, Miss Janet Barclay, and the Press Secretary, Miss Jane Amys, who worked tirelessly as members of the Conference staff. Above all, the Institute is grateful to its corporate and union subscribers without whom neither the Conference nor this book would be possible.

November, 1963   T.E.H.R.

CONTRIBUTORS

THOMAS BALOGH, Reader in Economics, Balliol College, Oxford; Adviser, British Labour Party

GREGORY G. BAUM, Associate Professor of Theology, St. Michael's College, University of Toronto; Member, Vatican Secretariat for Christian Unity

JEAN ETHIER-BLAIS, Professeur, Faculté des Lettres, Université de Montréal; Literary Critic of *Le Devoir*

BERTRAND DE JOUVENEL, Président-Directeur Général de la Société d'Etudes et de Documentation Economiques Industrielles et Sociales, Paris

KASPAR D. NAEGELE, Professor of Sociology, Department of Anthropology and Sociology, University of British Columbia

C. WILLIAM NICHOLLS, Professor of Religious Studies, University of British Columbia; Adviser, World Council of Churches

RONALD S. RITCHIE, Director, Imperial Oil Limited; Chairman, 1963 Couchiching Conference

GIOVANNI SARTORI, Professor of Sociology and Associate Professor of Political Science, University of Florence

FRANK H. UNDERHILL, Historian and Political Commentator

ELISEO VIVAS, The John Evans Professor of Moral and Intellectual Philosophy, Northwestern University

CONTENTS

Preface	v
Contributors	vii
Values in Conflict RONALD RITCHIE	3
The Crisis in Human Values FRANK UNDERHILL	12
Personal Freedom and Social Responsibility BERTRAND DE JOUVENEL	21
Conflicts within Society KASPAR NAEGELE	28
Social Injustice and Rational Reform THOMAS BALOGH	42
Scriptural Faith and Cultural Values GREGORY BAUM	50
God and the Value Scale WILLIAM NICHOLLS	58
The Political Meaning of Liberty and Equality GIOVANNI SARTORI	65
Democracy and Nationalism: The Canadian Conflict FRANK UNDERHILL	71
The Validity of Prevailing Economic Values THOMAS BALOGH	79

A Comment
    JEAN ETHIER-BLAIS   89

The Revolution in Personal Values
    ELISEO VIVAS   92

On Personal Moral Values
    JEAN ETHIER-BLAIS   112

Selected Bibliography   125

Board of Directors   131

Publications   132

VALUES

When Alice came out of the Duchess's kitchen she saw the Cheshire Cat who was perched on the limb of a tree above her and was smiling a broad smile. "Cheshire Puss", she enquired, "would you tell me, please, which way I ought to walk from here?" "That depends a good deal on where you want to get to", said the Cat. "I don't care much where—" said Alice. "Then it doesn't matter which way you walk," said the Cat. "—so long as I get somewhere," *Alice added as an explanation. "Oh, you're sure to do that," said the Cat, "if you only walk long enough." With which judicial summation of the problem, the Cheshire Cat slowly vanished from view until nothing visible was left of him save the broad smile on his face.*

The Wonderland in which Alice found herself had a good many resemblances to the difficult world in which we are living today. There seemed to be no established rules or standards of conduct; and the longer Alice stayed there, the more perplexing it became as to what system of values held this strange society together. As was explained to her, you had to keep running in order to stay in the same place. Each individual used words in his own special particular sense; for long periods of time each seemed to live a completely self-centred, almost solipsistic existence. And in the background there was always the harsh voice of the Queen shouting "Off with their heads". In the end Alice decided that they were all only a pack of cards, quite meaningless, though interesting and provoking for a dreamlike hour or so.

FRANK UNDERHILL

VALUES IN CONFLICT

RONALD RITCHIE

Western man is at war with himself. That he is so at war is, for some, a source of frustration, confusion, and despair. It can also be a source of hope. This civil "cold war," this uncertainty and frustration, are part of man's endless quest for values by which the individual and his society can live and grow.

At various times and places in human history, the search for values has been relatively quiescent. Societies have been, for periods sometimes long but usually short, nearly static. During such periods, men have lived with sets of values which were widely accepted within their society and more or less appropriate to their level of knowledge and their ways of life. Such periods of relatively stable value systems have always been interrupted by some force of change—abruptly or gradually and with gathering force. The force has sometimes been external, sometimes internal. Such forces of change always bring conflict in the arena of values. Long-accepted values are thrown into question. The differences between what men believe and what they do are shown up in stark relief, and the demands for new values to suit the new needs of new social situations become both challenges and sources of confusion and despair.

The Renaissance and the Reformation launched such forces and such periods of change. Their impacts on the value systems of our Western world are not even yet fully worked out. Behind much of our present conflict and uncertainty in the field of values, however, lie also the forces of that complex, interrelated series of changes which we loosely call "The Industrial Revolution." Over the past two centuries, it has touched, disrupted, even re-created almost every aspect of life in the Western world. It is still doing so, and is now rapidly throwing up sweeping challenges to the social structures and value systems of the whole of the rest of the world besides.

The forces and process of change labelled the Industrial Revolution provide a particularly instructive example of how changes in one sphere of human life, in this case, the economic, can sweep change through all others—the political, the social, the ethical, and the religious—tumbling and changing value systems in their wake. The industrial revolution has done much more than change the ways in which men work together to produce goods and services on one hand, and to extend the range and variety of their choices at the level of consumption on the other. Important as continuing change in production and consumption has been for value systems, its direct effect does not reveal the total picture. For instance, the purely economic and technological changes made both possible and necessary central governments whose sway would be more pervasive and effective at the local level. With increased social mobility as a by-product of both new productive systems and higher levels of consumption, the power and influence of the local community became less important and less real, while that of the central and more remote government became more determining. Man's ideas of the politically good and the politically practical are in flux as a result.

Western man has been swept along by a second revolution whose end is not yet in sight: the scientific revolution. These two revolutions are, of course, inextricably interrelated. In its origin, the industrial revolution is predominantly a revolution of technology and, as such, one of the fruits of the scientific revolution. Through the work of its Darwins, its Freuds, and its Einsteins, the scientific revolution has transformed man's perception of his universe and of himself. Like a hurricane lashing the trees of a forest, it has attacked his value systems, tearing some up by the roots, sweeping many into the debris of history, and leaving those that remain to grow in new and different ways.

Today, the effects of these shattering blows to established value systems are not to be observed only or even principally in the speculations and ways of life of a small elite in Western society. The questioning, the uncertainty, and the resolution of value conflicts touch the lives, the attitudes, and the faiths of all. Because the industrial revolution increasingly widens horizons, opens opportunities for choice, provides more geographic, social, and economic mobility, and inexorably involves each man in widening multiplicity of relationships with other men, personal and impersonal, more men than ever before are not only affected, but realize that they are affected. To keep our society from flying apart or from lapsing into apathetic disbelief, it is therefore important that our conflicts in values be seen in perspective by a much larger proportion of our society than, in other times, has usually been concerned with such questions. In a rapidly changing society, mere acceptance is irrelevant and inadequate. There must be a continuous search for understanding and for the ingredients of a new synthesis. This may mean that old values die and new ones rise to take their place. More often, it means that old values come to be seen in new perspective and with new dimensions. It can, indeed, be a synthesis of growth.

What, then, are some of the principal value-system conflicts in our Western society today, and is it possible to discern some of the likely directions of the new synthesis? This brief paper makes no pretensions to a definitive charting, and its dimensions would not permit this even if such a project were within its writer's competence. Its aim is the much simpler one of highlighting some of the more obvious areas of conflict, areas in which the rapid evolution of our institutions and of our problems have led to paradoxes in our thinking which not all have recognized, and fewer have resolved.

A central element in Western value systems is the individual: his position, his needs, his rights in relation to others, and his obligations to them. Wars and revolutions have been launched and fought to secure or to defend his political liberty, his freedom of worship, his economic wellbeing. Political ideologies and political parties claim the individual as their basic concern, and in his name often promote programmes for regimenting him. Moral codes centre on the role and the rights of the individual, and religions proclaim ideal standards for his relationship with other men and with God. The actual and the proclaimed place of the individual in our society and in our systems of values should, therefore, be a fruitful place in which to search for values in conflict in our Western society.

Let us begin with the political sphere. The twentieth century confronts man with political threats to his freedom which are far more subtle, and perhaps far more serious, than those which prompted the wars, revolutions, and constitutional reforms that make up the history of his pursuit of political liberty. The threat is more subtle because it comes through the political instruments which are theoretically *his* instruments, because it comes in the name of objectives which are as much his objectives as is political liberty. The threat is more serious in its potentialities because there is today no agreed and limited sphere of action and concern allocated to governments. Increasingly, the efforts of the state have no limit, and it becomes the final arbiter in more and more of man's relations with his fellow man, and even in much of his way of life. To "render unto Caesar the things that are Caesar's and unto God the things that are God's" becomes an increasingly one-sided proposition.

These twentieth-century threats in the political sphere have many manifestations. Our system of representative democracy had its origins in a desire to check the arbitrary power of rulers. It was the arbitrariness of the power rather than its extent which was the main danger to be guarded against. As the industrial revolution has changed the world in which we live, and brought even more subjects into the sphere of government, our system of representative democracy has, without its forms being altered, come to be more nearly a periodic delegation of almost unchecked power. With the ever-widening range of the government's role and with the complexity of the issues at stake, this periodic delegation—through elections—can be considered less and less as even an electoral judgment on policies and priorities. At times, it comes perilously close to being a simple plebiscite verdict on leaders.

This same complexity and range of government activity and responsibility inevitably leads to a very large role for a growing public service—the bureaucracy, as it is invidiously called. If direct democracy protected the liberty of the individual in the Greek city states (a thesis which the record of history does not always support), and if representative democracy protected the free man from the arbitrary actions of kings and autocrats, can we still be sure that it gives him real protection in a day when his rulers, elected and appointed, speak with greater voice and authority because they speak in his name and on a range of subjects whose intricacies and implications he cannot hope to comprehend. It was Montesquieu who said that the abuse of power is greatest when laws do not anticipate it. How the laws should anticipate it, in a day when the role of government knows no fixed bounds, and its activities must involve so many kinds of expertise, is not a question which is easy to answer.

Another manifestation of the threat to the political liberty of the individual can be seen in the ever-growing tendency toward big government in the geographic sense. Local governments and school boards more and more give way to provincial and state governments. Provincial and state governments more and more give way, willingly or no, to central governments at the national level. In some spheres, national governments show signs of giving way to the governments of regional communities of nations. Many speak longingly of world government, usually with no very clear spelling out of either roles or net advantage.

In none of this is there a conspiracy to limit individual liberty or the responsiveness of governments to those whom they govern. In part, there is simply a response to the economic and political needs of a more interrelated world. In part, there is a misplaced faith in our ability to meet complex needs and solve complex problems by imposing simple answers on a large scale. In part, there is the paradox of impatience, even intolerance, of the right of individuals or groups to be different, co-existing with professed belief in political systems based on the value of the individual and his right to political liberty.

It is clear, then, that in the political sphere, our Western society does have unresolved value conflicts. It is clear, too, that it has not yet arrived at a fully satisfactory reconciliation between, on the one hand, the value it professes to place upon individual liberty and, on the other, the fact of exceedingly intricate problems of government in an increasingly complex society. Even in the best of all possible worlds, we would find ourselves living with an uneasy balance between liberty and justice, between freedom and equality. The danger which faces us today is that the desirable balance may be lost, that liberty may disappear in fact while its forms survive, that even representative democracy may become more total in its concerns and in its demands than is appropriate to the complexity of our society and the minimum requirements of liberty and justice.

In the economic sphere, too, the place of the individual is a fruitful standpoint from which to test our value systems and their consistency. Whatever else the industrial revolution may have done, it is clearly demonstrated in North America, in Western Europe, and even in Soviet Russia, that it has vastly increased the potential economic well-being of all members of a society, and opened up to them a much wider choice in their way of life. It can continue to do so.

Many contend that, while giving the individual whole new dimensions of liberty in this fashion, it has simultaneously involved him in worse forms of slavery than he had previously known. They argue that, for many men, the productive process has become a soul-destroying monotony, a form of slavery to the pay cheque and the machine; or, alternatively, that for most, freedom of choice is an illusion, that it is invalidated by the machinations of selfish men who apply the "hidden persuaders." Still again, they decry the slavery of Western men to a crass materialism that is continuously reinforced by the needs of the productive system. In short, they argue that in the economic sphere, man has sold his birthright for a mess of pottage, and that here, at least, in our Western society our faith in the value of the individual finds no reflection in our economic arrangements.

That the technology of the continuing industrial revolution poses problems in the sphere of human values is unquestionable. It will almost certainly continue to do so. It will continually create new circumstances which ensure that no given solution can be continually appropriate. A central issue is whether the needs of the industrial process can be reconciled with human needs, with the need to find satisfaction and growth in work. If material well-being requires many men to lead a less than fully human life while on the job, it seems a rather high price to pay for it. This is not to overlook the vast improvements in the physical environment and physical demands of most work. In our Western economies today, work, even for the mass of men, less frequently involves serious hardship and discomfort. Nor does it as often involve burdensome physical labour or unhealthy working conditions. Less frequently, too, than in the past, does it mean autocratic bosses and unnatural subservience. But still, for many men, it is in an important sense less than fully human. It does not challenge their capacities; it does not require or encourage growth.

More and more industrial leaders, labour leaders, and other interested thinkers are beginning to question whether this state of affairs is inevitable. Certainly, if there is a solution, it is not one which will yield simply to goodwill. Real questions of interest, capacity, organization, and technology are involved. Certainly, with the question coming to be more widely studied, the chances of solution are better. It is possible that as solutions are found, they will solve more than conflicts in our value system. It may well be discovered that, at the same time, they may reduce (although no one should expect them to eliminate) some very human conflicts at the industrial level.

Setting aside the discussion of the nature of work itself, let us examine the degree to which there is *liberty* for the individual in the economic sphere of our industrialized Western society. Certainly, if freedom be taken to require the possibility of choice, then most people in our North American society have this requisite to a greater degree at the economic level than in any other society in history. They have it as consumers, they have it in career opportunities, and they have it in geographic mobility. Such choice is much more real when most people's income resources are well above the minimum requirements of subsistence, and when the educational opportunities which make career choice a reality are widely available. Both of these requisites are increasingly met.

There are those who argue that, in the mass, men do not take good advantage of such choice as is available to them, and that, in fact, they are prevented by the crass, materialistic motives of a few profit-dominated men from doing so. Concealed behind an often genuinely felt concern for the well-being of the many, such statements often hide what is really an arrogant contempt for the ordinary man, together with an over-simplified view of the processes of social change and of the way in which men's capacity to deal with new situations develops. The opportunity for wider choice and fuller growth is, after all, a relatively new one in our society. Yet no very painstaking historical assessment is necessary to demonstrate that there is already a heartening growth in the breadth of interest, depth of understanding, and level of taste of a steadily widening proportion of the population.

As one battle for liberty is won, however, the prize seems always to be threatened from another quarter—very often, it seems, from a quarter which helped bring the earlier victory. So it is today that, in the economic sphere, individual freedom may now, in some ways, be threatened in our society by both trade unions and governments. It has often been argued that trade unions have not really advanced the economic interests of labour beyond what would have come automatically from the pressures of the market-place. Whatever the merits of this argument, it is certainly clear that unions once had the very important function of helping large masses of labouring men to feel less defenceless, isolated, and powerless than they once were. There is, however, a strange parallel here with the tendencies in representative democracy already referred to. Instruments which men appear to control, and which appear to be designed only to advance their interests, can demand loyalty and unquestioning obedience beyond that which any purely external instrument can exact. Once again, Montesquieu's dictum may be relevant: "The abuse of power is greatest when laws do not anticipate it."

Government, too, has been seen as an instrument for promoting freedom and equity in the economic sphere. Inevitably, as the web of men's economic relationships has grown more intricate and spread wider, government has become more and more involved in it. The trend has been accentuated by the entry of governments on a growing range of welfare activities. Inevitably, some sacrifice of liberty, some limitation on freedom of individual choice, and that not only for the economically elite, results. Governments cannot accept responsibility without regulating. They must hedge, restrict, and direct, to achieve their social welfare purposes. In a sense, it is somewhat anomalous, at a stage in our economic and social development when disparities in income have been drastically reduced by progressive income taxes and otherwise, when we speak of our society as affluent because the material standard of living for most men in it is higher than even the privileged have enjoyed through most of humanity's history—that at such a stage we should be putting even more stress on centrally directed welfare measures for all. The questions raised here are really questions of degree and balance. Certainly we would be unwise to expect answers to be uniform for all societies and all times.

In the economic sphere, then, there are elements very similar to those we have already observed in the political sphere. It seems doubtful whether we have been able to achieve a full reconciliation, certainly not a final one, between the apparent needs of an exceedingly complex society and the value which we give to the individual, between liberty and equity. In striving for this reconciliation, this balance, we tend to have a too simple enthusiasm for uniformity and the utility of centrally imposed formulae, too little appreciation of the values of diversity and the effectiveness of plural decision-making. We tend, perhaps too often, to forget a truth which has been well expressed by Lionel Trilling: "Some paradox of our natures leads us, when once we have made our fellow men the objects of our enlightened interest, to go on to make them the objects of our pity, then of our wisdom, ultimately of our coercion."[1]

In terms of the value sector we have chosen to probe, can we find, in those parts of the social sphere which extend beyond the basically political and economic, more consistency, less confusion, in our value systems in Western society today? Man can scarcely be visualized as other than a social animal, a product of his society. His every thought and action are conditioned by the social facts of his existence. We would expect, then, to find the individual subjected to a variety of social influences, forces, pressures. Are these, in our society, consistent with the value which we profess to place upon the individual, his freedom, his possibilities of self-fulfilment?

Perhaps the readiest evidence of conflict is found in the fact that we do not seem to find it easy to make up our mind where the balance should lie between the individual opportunity to be different and the egalitarian compulsion to be uniform. The pressures for conformity are widespread and inescapable, and they often have a ready ally in the desire of the individual to be accepted. As Tocqueville pointed out long ago, democracies have a built-in tendency toward totalitarianism. Much as a group may, in some respects, value him, it feels uneasy about and distrusts the superior individual or the individual who is merely different. Often this distrust is carried to the point of ensuring that he has limited opportunity to show or profit from his superiority or his difference. Some attitudes toward education, prevalent for many years in North America and more recently in the United Kingdom as well, offer a commonplace illustration of the innate desire to equate equality with uniformity, to limit opportunity for the individual in the interests of levelling down.

It is not easy, at this time, to make a convincing case for optimism

[1] *The Liberal Imagination*, New York, 1957, p. 215.

about the future in these areas of the social sphere, and yet perhaps some optimism is justified. Perhaps there is even a smattering of evidence on the scene today to support optimism. As the range of choice and of opportunity grows for more and more in the material area and, therefore, in the intellectual and aesthetic areas, we may develop a somewhat greater degree of tolerance and even approval of diversity. As more and more people come to have a little better appreciation of our society in all of its complexities, perhaps we shall have a little more appreciation of the value of diversity and a little less confidence in the benefits of imposed simplicity.

Values are in conflict in our Western society. They will continue to be so. This is a mark of a changing society. The scientific and industrial revolutions alone, during the past two centuries, have been of such extent, such breadth and depth, and such an accelerating pace right up to the present moment that it would be surprising indeed if our systems of thought and belief about values had been able to keep pace. It is less a question of scrapping fundamental values which have been evolved laboriously over the centuries, than of seeing them in new dimensions, of working out their meanings in the light of a new society and new knowledge, both of infinitely greater extent and complexity than our forefathers have known at any time and place.

In this continuing task of identification, reconciliation, and synthesis, a task which must touch more men than ever before in history, there are difficulties and hazards. Our society is complicated, and the facts with which it must contend are equally so. Man's most important accomplishments rest on his intellectual ability to abstract and to simplify, to find order in what at first seems hopelessly chaotic—but there is an offsetting danger in this ability. Abstractions which are tools of thought can come to have an over-simplified pseudo-reality of their own, can come, indeed, to be objects of loyalty and emotional fervour which can dangerously mislead. We believe, we say, in the importance of the individual, in the need for him to have the opportunity to grow and develop for his own self-realization, subject only to the equal need of those around him. Yet, in a complex society such as ours, where the most important enemies are, in a sense, internal, the individual constantly faces the subtle threat of being overwhelmed by his own instruments in the interests of abstractions. That conflicts in values should be recognized—and a balance be sought—is his surest protection.

THE CRISIS IN HUMAN VALUES

FRANK UNDERHILL

The Couchiching Conference has chosen a difficult subject. We are dealing not with such simple problems as Russia or Latin America or Africa or the United States or Big Business or Mass Communication, but with what has been going on in our own minds during the past generation, with our conception of the nature of man and his relation to the society in which he lives.

Everywhere nowadays one hears it said that the ideals by which men used to regulate their lives, the values according to which they lived, the purposes which they tried to achieve individually and collectively, have disintegrated in our modern generation. Our present-day confusions and frustrations are ultimately due to the fact that we no longer feel any certainty as to where we are going or ought to be going. This uncertainty shows itself in the weakening of traditional religious sanctions, in the agonizing self-torture which so many individuals experience, in the difficulties which the younger generation have in adjusting themselves in the world of their elders, in the rootlessness of which so many are conscious in the midst of our contemporary North American civilization, in the futility of our politics—local, national, and international. It is about all this confusion and frustration—religious, intellectual, moral, and aesthetic—that we shall be talking.

I am not a very suitable person to introduce a discussion of this kind. My chief disqualification is that I am too old. I spent the first ten years of my life in the reign of Queen Victoria. I believe that he who did not live before 1914 can never know what the sweetness of life is. As a Victorian I was born a liberal, an optimist, a rationalist. But the younger people who are most concerned with these problems of values are, of course, all anti-liberal, pessimistic, and irrational.

I grew up believing, with my pre-1914 generation, that "liberalism" is the most satisfactory word that can be found to describe the best and finest in our Hellenic-Judaeo-Christian inheritance. But just because it did sum up so well the ideals of the pre-1914 generation in Western Europe and America, liberalism today has become a general term of abuse.

Perhaps, however, liberalism is in such disfavour today as a philosophy because it has been so successful in practice over the last two centuries in realizing so many of its ideals.

Liberalism means generally the inheritance of the spirit of the Enlightenment of the eighteenth century. The Enlightenment was the spirit which had arisen out of the Renaissance and Reformation of the fifteenth and sixteenth centuries and the scientific revolution of the seventeenth century. In politics it expressed itself in the American Declaration of Independence: "We hold these truths to be self-evident, that all men are created equal, that they are endowed by their Creator with certain unalienable rights, that among these are Life, Liberty and the pursuit of Happiness." And it expresses itself again in the famous trinity of the French Revolution: "Liberty, Equality, Fraternity." The essence of man, according to this belief, is that he is a rational creature; and, because all men share in this capacity for rationality, they share in a fundamental human dignity, which is what is meant by saying that they are all equal. Man is capable of progress through the exercise of his reason, he makes his own history, he is in principle indefinitely perfectible. The word "Enlightenment" signifies the intellectual emancipation, which the men of the eighteenth century had so happily reached, from the domination of the individual's mind by religion and of human society by religious wars.

Every eighteenth-century man was potentially a *philosophe*. The ideal society toward which they were moving was the civilization of the dialogue, a dialogue among scientists and philosophers in which every man would be trained by an enlightened education to take part. The hero of the eighteenth century was that ideal rationalist, Isaac Newton, who had elucidated the fundamental principle underlying physical nature. "Nature and nature's laws lay hid in night,/God said 'Let Newton be' and there was light." And future rationalistic Newtons would bring similar light to the study of human nature and human societies.

This eighteenth-century society of the *philosophes* was a secular society, as distinct from the sacramental society which the Christian Church has been trying for centuries to establish. The evangel, the good news which it brought to man, was that he might be saved not by the intervention of some supernatural power but by his own efforts to live in accordance with nature. It was also, therefore, individualistic. In England, as Voltaire discovered to his delight, every man went to heaven in his own way.

Today, of course, this Enlightenment ideology is a subject for savage derision or condescending mirth. Any university sophomore can tear to pieces its liberal delusions, its superficial insight into human nature and human society, its naive ignoring of the problem of evil, its blindness toward the past, its utopian millennialist confidence in the future, the unpardonable if largely unconscious *hubris* of its humanist faith in man. Today pessimism has replaced optimism. Today imaginative secular thinkers write not Utopias but Dystopias—*Brave New World, Nineteen Eighty-Four*. He is a very daring optimist who ventures to express the opinion that the future is uncertain.

Today the religious thinker who has most influenced the attitude of thoughtful North Americans toward contemporary social and political problems, Reinhold Niebuhr, writes about "The Irony of American History." He takes his own America as the theme of his sermon because it was in America that the Enlightenment faith spread most widely and penetrated most deeply; and accordingly the present-day disillusionment and frustration of his countrymen over the role of the United States in the world stimulate him to an ironical insight into what was inadequate in the whole ideology of the Enlightenment. So what Niebuhr's neo-orthodox religion offers us in politics is a pessimistic liberalism—surely a contradiction in terms. How can you be liberal if you believe that man is a poor sinful creature, his reason always liable to corruption through his inherent selfishness, his capacity for love and compassion toward his fellow men always poisoned by his own imperial ambitions? Yet it is to this severely chastened sceptical liberalism that any mature, thoughtful, sophisticated liberal seems to be driven today.

One result is that we are failing to display a dynamic unifying faith in any system of Western values with which we can confront the challenge of the Communist faith.

Why has the dynamic optimistic faith in man which characterized the Enlightenment broken down in the two centuries since the *philosophes* were at their height? Why are we in such confusion today as to what our real values are or ought to be? The various speakers at this conference will be presenting a variety of reasons based on their own special interest as scholars and thinkers. And I am not competent enough in philosophy, in psychology, in economics, in sociology, in literary criticism, to try to anticipate them.

Since I am an historian, I should like to pause here for a few minutes in order to draw your attention to two historians who have discussed these matters. Our proceedings for the next few days are going to be mostly concerned with the ideas in men's heads, and a good deal of the discussion will therefore be rather abstract. The virtue of the historian is his interest in concrete events. I think that the ordinary inquisitive layman is likely to learn more about the values in conflict in our generation from reading good historians who try to trace out the subtle connections between ideas and events, than from reading social scientists or philosophers or theologians with all their system-making.

My first historian I have picked in order to illustrate the fact that our confusions and conflicts in values today are not something new or unique in this generation. They were anticipated in the contradictions and the ambiguities of the values within the society of our grandfathers. One of the things that you learn from history is that every generation of men is always going through a period of painful, critical, and destructive transition; and another is that society can stand a lot of ruin.

In 1941 Professor Carleton J. H. Hayes of Columbia published a volume in the historical series *The Rise of Modern Europe*. The period covered by his volume was that of the years 1871 to 1900, and he called the book *A Generation of Materialism*. Professor Hayes wrote as an American Catholic who had grown up and acquired his own personal values in this generation with which he was now dealing as an historian; and this gives his chapters a poignancy not to be found in most historical writing. He confessed in his preface that the volume as it was could hardly have been written till his old age because he had grown up seeing these last three decades of the nineteenth century as "a glorious stage in the progress of European and Western civilization toward ever greater liberty, democracy, social betterment and scientific control of nature." "I still see these decades thus," he goes on, "but I also now see them even more clearly, as a fertile seed-time for the present (1941) and quite different harvest of personal dictatorship, social degradation and mechanized destruction. It is this dual character of the age, at once the climax of enlightenment and the source of disillusionment, which gives it peculiar interest and pregnant significance."

I commend Professor Hayes's volume, because, you see, here he is, putting the disintegration of the civilization of the Enlightenment back in the years 1871–1914. His last chapter is entitled "The Climax of the Enlightenment," and it is divided into three sections subtitled: (1) The Cult of Progress, (2) Great Expectations, (3) The Lurking Nemesis. He might have been writing about our present generation. Nearly everything that we shall be hearing in the next few days about our current intellectual, moral, and spiritual crisis, you can find discussed, at least by way of preface, in his book on *A Generation of Materialism, 1871–1900*. The crisis in human values which confronts each generation anew is never as new as it seems to that generation.

Of course the historian who has had the greatest direct, popular influence in North America is Arnold Toynbee. And he has shaken most of his readers by his prophetic denunciations of the values embodied in our "post-Christian" civilization. But Toynbee is not so highly regarded among scholars as among the readers of the Luce magazines, and so I pass him over. To historians he appears a highly subjective, somewhat capricious, theologian. To theologians he appears a highly subjective, somewhat capricious, historian.

My second historian is a younger man, Professor H. Stuart Hughes of Harvard. He wasn't born till 1916. He has been making a great name for himself of late in the field of intellectual history, and his special interest has been in the disintegration of the Enlightenment and the rise of new values in Europe from about 1890 to the present. Two of his recent works, *Consciousness and Society* (1958) and *Contemporary Europe: A History* (1961), are masterly treatments of the same kind of subject as that with which Professor Hayes dealt in his earlier volume on a slightly earlier period, *A Generation of Materialism, 1871–1900*.

Professor Hughes as a human being has himself been going through some of the agonizing reappraisals of his generation which he analyses in his histories of contemporary Europe. Last year he published a little book, *An Approach to Peace*, in which he throws over most of the orthodox American pieties and abandons the doctrines of the American Establishment about how to defend our Western liberal values against Russian totalitarianism. He has placed himself outside the consensus of his society. He is seeking a saving remnant among his people who will commit themselves to utopian policies, as a way of shocking his fellow citizens into a re-examination of how far their professed values are betrayed by their actual conduct. He made an initial try-out of his utopianism by running against the Kennedy and Lodge families for the seat of senator from Massachusetts. But, alas for utopian idealism, the Cuban crisis intervened just before the senatorial election. Still, for my tastes, Stuart Hughes remains the most attractive of all our modern utopians. He is so humble and modest and quiet as he sets out on his pilgrim's progress.

The book of Professor Hughes which first struck my attention was a little volume on Spengler which he published in 1950 (being then thirty-four years old). In this book he told how the idea for his *magnum opus* suddenly came to Spengler in Munich in 1911. He then proceeded to discuss the intellectual atmosphere of that year 1911 in which Spengler sat down to write his famous *Decline of the West*. He picked out four men, contemporaries of Spengler, who were to be, he said, the seminal thinkers for the next generation: Freud, Bergson, Pareto, and Sorel. By 1911, he said, these men had reached and published their final conclusions. And he pointed out how these four thinkers, and here I quote, "with their skepticism about the power of reason to control man's actions and their doubts of his capacity for moral and political progress, lived in a world far removed from the optimism and self-confidence of the popular writers, the men of affairs, and the leaders of parliamentary majorities of 1911."

Well, those remarks of Mr. Hughes brought me up short. For 1911 was the year in which I graduated from the University of Toronto. And it shocked me in the 1950's to reflect that of the four men picked out by Mr. Hughes as the intellectual fathers of that part of the twentieth century in which I would be living, I had in 1911, to the best of my recollection, heard of only one. That was Bergson. I have read Sorel since, but I haven't read a word of Pareto, and I have contented myself with absorbing Freud by osmosis. In 1911, though I thought of myself as a very modern sophisticated young intellectual, I shared all the illusions of the "popular writers, the men of affairs, the leaders of parliamentary majorities" of those days about which young Mr. Hughes of the next generation was somewhat contemptuous. I shared their optimism about the continuous upward progressive trend of our Western civilization, about the rationality of Western man, and his capacity to solve his deepest problems. The only way in which I have matured since then is that I no longer believe in man's capacity to solve his deepest problems, but I do believe in his capacity to live with them without becoming as neurotic as most of my younger friends are.

The significant fact, however, is that "the popular writers, the men of affairs, the leaders of parliamentary majorities" of 1963 are using the same language about the values of our Western civilization as their predecessors were using in 1911. Is this merely a performance of ritual on their part? Are they dishonest hypocrites? Or is it that we can't find better values because there aren't any better? Naturally, I incline to this last hypothesis. My battle-cry in assaulting the troubles of our day is "Back to the Enlightenment."

Those who are younger than me, however, might usefully employ some of their spare time by making out a list of the four or six men who they think will be recognized as the seminal thinkers for the next generation, that is, the generation from 1970 to 2000; the men who by now, 1963, have reached and published their final conclusions, and whose conclusions will determine the character of the thinking of the last generation of the twentieth century, the generation that will come just one hundred years after that Generation of Materialism about which Professor Carleton Hayes wrote. If they save this list until they are well into that next generation, they may then consult it to find out how deeply they saw beneath the surface trends of the generation of the 1940's, 1950's, and 1960's.

There is one other point to be noted about the writings of Professors Hayes and Hughes. They were both dealing with intellectual developments in Europe rather than in their own America. The disintegration of the ideology of the Enlightenment has not gone as far on this continent as on the other side of the Atlantic. We have not been swept by the demonic destructive mass passions which erupted in the age of Hitler; we have had no revolutions in North America since the age of the Enlightenment. We have gone through no such traumas as the European peoples of our day have experienced. We fought our twentieth-century wars thousands of miles overseas. We maintain at least a general formal devotion to habitual religious beliefs. Neither Marxism nor Stalinism nor Fascism has made much impact here. And the United States in its Declaration of Independence, its Bill of Rights, its Constitution, still speaks an eighteenth-century language which makes its pronouncements about democracy and liberty sound strangely old-fashioned to European and Asiatic and African ears.

As for Canada, we never had an eighteenth century—which is one of the things wrong with us. French Canada was a society founded by leaders of the seventeenth-century Counter-Reformation. English Canada was just being founded at the end of the eighteenth century by men who rejected enlightenment doctrines about life, liberty, and the pursuit of happiness. This, of course, does not matter much because we are not undertaking the responsibility of leading the twentieth-century world forward into the eighteenth century, and we watch these spiritual agonies of our overseas and American contemporaries largely as spectators.

But in one respect the United States has gone further into the twentieth century than anyone else. She has taken the lead in one development which has gone far to undermine the values of the Enlightenment and in which she has become the model that all other Western communities are following. This is the emergence of the civilization of mass democracy.

The United States plunged into mass democracy more than a hundred years ago when Jacksonian democracy swept over the country. Mass democracy, as distinguished from Jeffersonian democracy, is that equalitarian form of society in which no one recognizes the leadership of any superior elite group in politics, in morality, in taste, in culture generally. The ordinary man feels no need to stretch his imagination, discipline his intellect, refine his sensibilities, beyond the mediocre standards to which he has been accustomed. But his aptitude for technological invention produces an economy of mass production for a mass market in which the consumers become as standardized as the product they consume. In such a society, the autonomous individual idealized by the Enlightenment tends to disappear.

We should note that it is the massive size and complexity of our modern technology that today tend to undermine the individuality of the individual, not capitalism as such or socialism as such. His society is too complex for him to understand, he feels himself further and further removed from the centre of power, he is tempted to retire to a purely private life. The liberties of the responsible citizen which the Enlightenment handed down to him become unreal. As Aldous Huxley has put it, "never were so many manipulated so much by so few." Those two great inventions of the modern American genius, Hollywood and Madison Avenue, will probably do more in the long run to corrupt and debase the Enlightenment ideal of the rational, responsible, independent citizen than all the Hitlers and Stalins.

I seem to be turning into a pessimist. Yet I seem to detect a ray of light in the darkness. I have confessed how unfounded was the optimism which possessed most of my generation just before 1914. But perhaps the pessimism, the defeatism, the despair, the death-wish, which have obsessed the generation of the 1940's and 1950's will turn out to be equally unjustified. Perhaps, in the test-ban treaty signed this week in Moscow, the world has just turned a corner toward a new liberalism.

We should remind ourselves of the conditions out of which the Age of Enlightenment emerged. It suddenly dawned on European intellectuals sometime about the middle of the seventeenth century that they had become bored with the wars of religion. The struggles between Catholics and Protestants no longer seemed of such absorbing significance as they had seemed. At about the same time the thousand-year struggle between Christianity and Islam lost most of its drive. These questions which had aroused so much passion were not settled; they were simply abandoned as having become irrelevant and uninteresting to active minds. There were so many interesting intellectual pursuits to which intelligent men could turn, especially natural science and the study of man in society. And so the Age of Enlightenment began. Men believed again that they were rational creatures because they began to behave as such.

Today, likewise, we are perhaps approaching the moment when it will dawn on most intelligent men and women that they have become bored with our wars of religion—on both sides of the Iron Curtain. Not necessarily morally outraged, just bored. And they will turn to other, more creative activities. Perhaps younger people are going to live on into a second Age of Enlightenment. If so, they will surprise themselves by becoming what the men of my generation were—at least what we were when I was a young man before 1914, or at least what we thought we were. Believe it or not, they also will become capable of being liberal, optimistic, and rational.

PERSONAL FREEDOM AND SOCIAL RESPONSIBILITY

BERTRAND DE JOUVENEL

The relation between the individual and society cannot, I believe, be understood without taking into account the dimension of time. It is a surprising trait of the eighteenth-century philosophers to whom we owe our modes of thought that the Man they discuss seems never to have been a child. It is said that he is born free, while it is obvious that he is born helpless: man appears as a screaming infant, utterly incapable of ensuring his own survival, with his development depending upon the *sine qua non* condition of care and tuition lavished upon him for many years.

The continuation of any living species depends upon its solving the problem of rearing its young: a problem which is set more directly to the parents, and in more difficult terms, as we go up the ladder from the simplest to the most complex organisms. In the lowest orders of life, the new-born require no parental care: either as in parthenogenesis, they are born adult and self-supporting, or, as in seeding, wind or water carry them, or enough of them, into favourable environments where they develop of themselves. But as we go up the ladder of human forms, the young need more and longer protection and nurture from their parents. It is the striking order of Providence that what is meant for the highest perfection is the most vulnerable in its beginnings, and that the moral excellence of parental love and dedication is a biological requirement. Again we may say that the more complex the organism to be matured, the more organization it requires for its fostering. It is not enough that the natural parents should be attentive: to ensure against hazards, a coalition of parents needs to be formed. This coalition indeed might dissolve after a given crop of young was brought to adulthood, if no juniors had been procreated during that period; but, in the case of human beings, the rhythm of procreation is much shorter than the period of maturation, and therefore the association has to be permanent. It is under these conditions alone that language can develop.

The appearance of what we call a Man is unthinkable without a well-established fostering group, and we may therefore take it for certain that such association was achieved by whatever beings were our distant ancestors, long before they presented the features deserving the name Man. The question "How did man produce Society?" is therefore meaningless: it is Society which has produced Man.

This must have been a long and difficult process. From the evidence of anthropology, it appears that the rudest groups have great difficulty in bringing to adulthood an adequate number of their young: some such groups must therefore have dwindled and disappeared, while the most steadfast and efficient in attention and co-operation multiplied and populated the earth. We who live today are the fruits of such sustained endeavour, and no man may, without childish presumption, call himself "self-made." When any one of us draws up his balance of debits and credits with Society, he should not forget to inscribe therein that he is indebted to Society for his very life and faculty of expression.

Indeed we owe everything to society: and most unjust is the individual who does not feel that he owes his utmost efforts to society in return. But it is all too easy to draw from this glaring truth a dangerous falsehood. Men of such outstanding excellence as Albert Einstein or Yehudi Menuhin, just like the rest of us, had a fundamental debt to society: does this mean that their debt had to be discharged to the society of Nazi Germany, and that they should have acquitted this debt in whatever terms the leader of that society, Adolf Hitler, chose to state? This is an extreme instance, but it serves to bring out sharply the enormous fallacy arising from any personification of society.

What we are at this moment, we are thanks to the direct care of our educators. Our gratitude must go further back to all those who have contributed to build our material set and our culture. And as our gratitude must stretch far up to our natural and spiritual fosterers, so should our returns stretch far down, not to our children alone, but to the children of others and the following generations. This dual relationship is then one which implies great temporal depth: while it cannot be ignored without injustice, also it cannot without injustice be flattened into a mere contemporary relation. It is not true that the ruler of the day, or the ruling group, or indeed the majority, stands for all those to whom I am beholden, and are legitimately entitled to state the nature of the return I should make. The teachings of Socrates would not be to us an enduring treasure, had he taught as his contemporaries demanded.

I have just spoken of two injustices: I think the problem of individualism can fruitfully be discussed in terms of these two injustices. Certainly the individual is unjust if he does not behave as a diligent and beneficial parent. Of course I do not mean that he must personally have and raise children. Socrates, Aquinas, Descartes, Vivaldi, Mozart, were childless: indeed most of the spiritual parents of our Western culture have been biologically barren. What I do mean is that all adult members of a society stand *in loco parentis* to the coming generation and the children as yet unborn, and must contribute to their inheritance. In any peasant community, a man is adjudged a waster if he does not leave to his children a farm in better condition than he received it: and this same idea is quite validly transposed to the national equipment as a whole, which each generation should leave improved. We are scandalized if an educated father does not see to it that his sons receive a good education, while we are sympathetic and helpful to that father who struggles to give his children a better education that he himself received: and the general promotion of education is rightly a major preoccupation of our society. These are but the more visible aspects of a general process of increasing the common inheritance. It is clear that our individual abilities to benefit our successors are very unequal, but some contribution thereto we must make, however slight, and the individual who makes none may be called a "dead-end." If, whatever the immense accumulation of past efforts which has gone into making him, he is not the source of the merest trickle to those who come after him, yes indeed he is a "dead-end." And any individualist doctrine which does not lay stress on this obligation to the future is a dead-end individualism.

It follows therefore that we must be harsh judges of ourselves in this respect: it does not follow that we may be hasty censors of our fellows. Assuredly we are very fallible in our judgments as to what can benefit the coming generations. Let me give a striking instance. Had I been a contemporary and friend of Pascal, I would have regarded it as guilty squandering of his God-given genius that he applied his mind to the problems arising from so contemptible an occupation as dice-gambling, and I would have chided him for such futility, not suspecting for a moment that therefrom would arise probability calculus to which all our sciences today are so greatly indebted!

But indeed contemporaries are not prone to regard an individual's performance in regard to the future: they are far more apt to assess it with reference to their present desires and wants. The social pressures to which an individual is subjected tend to fit his conduct to the present requirement of his contemporaries rather than to the future advantage of his successors. It is indeed necessary that we should by our daily labours pay the services we daily receive from our fellows; this is market balance; it is necessary that we should in our current conduct observe the rules conducive to peaceful and co-operative co-existence, it is necessary that we should display good fellowship and conviviality. But the demands of our present fellows may go so far as to jeopardize our services to the future.

The beautiful myth of the Flood will serve us well here. If Noah had been so absorbed in social activities that he had not found time to build his Ark, we would not be here! The myth points out that here the individual activity was essentially social, ensuring the future, while the sociability of Noah would have had anti-social consequences. I strongly suspect that the emphasis placed by American educationalists upon social activities in the student years goes against the best interests of society. It is not easy to achieve and maintain the concentration required to make the most of one's years of learning, and the spirit of conviviality is inimical to such concentration. I think also that the enriching friendships are those formed on the basis of a common intellectual interest, and that the encouragement of associations without such a basis tends to dull such interests, to evaporate such concentration.

Sociability and the service of society are very different things. I doubt whether we would have the works of Descartes if, instead of shutting himself up in a room for seven years, as he tells us, he had spent this time attending parties, or even seminars.

The more a man is occupied with some great and difficult purpose, the less he is available for company. Even if he does take time off for company, unless it be a company pertinent to his preoccupation, he will find his preoccupation setting a curtain between the company and himself; he will be distrait and cloddish. When I was a small child, I cultivated radishes; I was most eager to know what progress they were making, and therefore two or three times a day I paid calls upon them, and lifted them carefully out to inspect their growth: strangely enough the results were not satisfactory.

Beholden to the past, the individual must contribute to the future: that is a social obligation, natural in that it corresponds to the nature of the social process. If however the social obligation of the individual is interpreted in terms of a close adjustment of his efforts to what presently suits his fellows, such an understanding of social obligation may impede the services to the future, and lead to what I shall venture to call a dead-end sociability, or a dead-end socialism, as the case may be: social conformism may well go against the interests of society by a process stretching in time.

History is not very interesting unless we believe that man is in some sense perfectible. It does not seem presently plausible that we can bring man to live longer than the extreme span of the past: Plato lived to ninety years; but what we do know is that we have already gotten a far larger proportion of the human beings born to live through the natural span, and that is an achievement. Similarly it is doubtful whether we shall get better men than, say, Socrates, not to speak of saints. But we may and should aim at getting an increasing proportion of men to achieve the perfection of the human type. However, a problem arises therefrom: the excellent man used to be called *egregius*, a significant term, "he who emerges from the herd." It was understood that the *egregius* had to be handled with due respect to his originality. Our problem is to extend such treatment to an increasing proportion of highly developed personalities. Personally I would indeed regard the true meaning of democracy as the treatment of every man with this delicate regard for his uniqueness, as I do not believe that intellectual distinction, however valuable, is everything. But as against this, a society embracing ever-increasing numbers ever more closely integrated in vast organizations, calls for methods of "processing" which are in sharp contradiction with the special treatment of each individual recognized as a person.

But there is worse to be noted. While we are engaged in the intellectual promotion of our populations, we are also engaged in their moral demotion. Our great economic progress, which brings so pleasing an increase in the material condition of the people, is achieved by the integration of workers in vast organizations, with a high pyramid of command. It follows that the man whose grandfather, a poor farmer, had to make decisions, now as a well-paid worker is expected only to carry out instructions.

It was held against capitalism that while in a previous economic stage each worker or family had its own means of production, the concentration of such means in a few hands allowed the owner of such concentrated means to exploit the wage-earners he employed. Whatever truth may be in such allegations in conditions of economic under-development when a reserve army of unemployed weighs down the labour market, such exploitation of the wage-earner is surely not characteristic of advanced countries with full employment. But what is true is that the concentration of the means of production concentrates decision-making, not indeed in the hands of owners but in the hands of managers: and this is an inevitable concomitant of large organizations, whether you call them capitalist, public, socialist, or communist. Nor is there any effective recourse against this natural concentration of decision and responsibility, in a legal democratization of these organizations, that is, in giving the members thereof joint collective control of the organization. In the political realm citizens enjoy this collective right to direct public affairs; do they exercise it? Although we do not like to say it, we know full well that only a minute proportion of the citizenry in fact are continually attentive to the conduct of public affairs. And the value of democracy lies not, as was hoped, in the fact that each and every one participates in government, but in the different, though itself very valuable, fact that anyone who volunteers such interest can exercise it. However good this is, we are still left with the fact that the phenomena of concentration which are characteristic of modern society are attended by a concentration of decision-making and responsibility, with the majority of citizens content to enjoy the benefits of efficient organization and more eager to claim their share of individual benefit than to share the burden of decision and responsibility. Sometimes I wonder whether the modern citizen is not symbolized by the automobilist who wants from the market the best possible car, and from the public authorities the best possible road system, in order to enjoy his personal, private freedom as automobilist.

If this is the psychological disposition, then it can be said that the progress of society has led to greater emphasis on personal, private liberty. That this was the trend of the West was acutely perceived by Benjamin Constant and by Sismondi at the beginning of the nineteenth century. It means that the future progress of society depends upon the use which individuals make of this personal liberty. And here, it seems to me, arises the problem for modern society. Either the state must dictate to all the conduct conducive to future good, and that is the authoritarian trend, or the institutions must be heavily biased in favour of those individuals who use their personal freedom toward the production of future good. In economic terms it means that either the state must itself ensure capital accumulation or it must favour profit-makers who reinvest and reinvest in more desirable directions. Let me point out that equal treatment of profits whatever use is made of them is, regarding the future, irrational. Similarly, a forward-looking government, aware that the benefits of increasing leisure are afforded to all by the progress of our collective efficiency, cannot smile equally upon the spending of leisure in libraries and its spending in bars and bowling alleys: it is bound to tax the latter heavily in favour of the former. Again in education, it seems to me that the offering of opportunities to all, when interpreted in terms of future outcome, implies a proportioning of the public benefaction to the individual response.

In short the more society relies upon individual freedom, as I think it should, the more it must proportion its favour to the use made of such freedom. A forward-looking view does not allow us to treat as equal before the law, activities which carry very different consequences. The economist can here provide an indication, derived from the notion of external costs. A gossip sheet implies not a simple financial relation between buyer and seller, but external disutilities inflicted upon society; so does the pollution of water and air by factories which do not control their effluents; so does the manufacture and distribution of gambling machines; while on the contrary a scientific journal provides external benefits. It is not my mood to prohibit anything, but I feel that a society which as far as ours relies on the individual must severely penalize individual or private conduct which is inherently or incidentally destructive. This it can best do by merely charging to such activities the costs they inflict upon society. If, as I am told, detergents create a special problem for the rephasing of the water, then the cost of abating this nuisance should be charged to the detergent industry, not to the ordinary taxpayer.

To me the essence of a free society is that all trust each: but the counterpart of this trust is that each should do service to all, not solely to those who are now here but also, and mainly, to those who will come after him. A sense of moral responsibility for the future must haunt the individual and, in so far as his conduct affects the future unfavourably, he must bear material responsibility for it. There is much anxiety now about the future of personal freedom; it is well founded; a main cause thereof, in my eyes, is that we have not sufficiently discriminated between constructive and destructive behaviour, treating them equally, which is unjust, it being unjust to treat equally things which are unequal.

Each stage of civilization has its understanding of natural law. To our ancestors, natural law showed that each man having freely entered into society kept therein the rights he had before entry. We do not now believe that this corresponds to any reality. The nature of society to us is a process of the promotion of man; natural law therefore is a dual recognition that the society is good in so far as it promotes man, and that the individual's rights, while a recognition of his dignity, are to be exercised toward the increasing fulfilment of society's purpose, the further promotion of our successors. The dangers of such a shift are obvious enough; but I regard it as inevitable and, notwithstanding its dangers, on the whole desirable.

CONFLICTS WITHIN SOCIETY

KASPAR NAEGELE

Le cœur a ses raisons, que la raison ne connait pas (Pascal)

Conflict takes little searching.[1] We all can give endless examples of inner argument. We know the sense of divergence between what we want and what we have. We know the gap between what we feel and what we can say. We can chart, if we possess the courage, the vacillations in our moods and our directions. We have participated in quarrels and fights. At the time they seemed inescapable; in retrospect they often appear silly. If all this were not so, the discussion of values would have made no sense. Yet, though it makes eminent sense, true to itself it invites various kinds of contributions. We are, I take it, sustaining a *public* discussion as *private* individuals. We come representing ourselves, whatever other involvements we may bring as well.

I am concerned to do justice to the character of moral conflict within our relations to one another and hence within ourselves. I hope to reach out to some evidence, but I shall hide neither my own commitments nor my ignorance and doubts. The fragments of my vision, still anything but steadily clear, can someday coalesce, I fervently hope, into the lucid belief that there is a way of having individual freedom on a large scale. Such freedom would be freedom from too much fear. It would shoulder uncertainty. It would be the means of expressing modes of love and justice. The institutions necessary for implementing such love and justice

[1] At least, so I thought. But the charming wife of a colleague, on hearing the assignment occupying me, denied assuredly and briskly that she had any conflicts. She would admit only to fears: to a single fear, to be quite correct. She feared the death of us all—a premature death caused by the designs of man. I clung to my claim. I dealt with her denial by seeing her fear as part of our conflict over being alive. She laughed at that thought. The conversation changed. The assignment persists.

have yet to be created. Even when they are, there will still be anger, pain, misfortune, and the inner conflict without which our transformation from birth to death is probably impossible.

Everything I say here must remain incomplete, largely because I do not know how to say what I feel or think, but also because we are dealing with a huge subject. Besides, as far as possible I wish alike to be just to what is and to what can be. I wish to be just to the facts in the deep sense of that word.

If we saw, heard, and felt everything, what would we have to report about the conflicts within Canadians? Would we see these conflicts outweigh or outweighed by delights and laughter, good times and well being? What would we conclude about the relations between the pain of conflict and the enjoyment of living? More immediately relevant: what could we say about the relation between the ways in which social patterns are sustained and the conflicts that irk, paralyse, or enrich Canadians?

Even our joint formulations within this volume will not quite do justice to our limited sense of the facts. We hardly represent the full range of the varieties of struggle and mastery which this country contains in any one day. Rather, we belong to those who have been bitten by self-consciousness. Increasingly this will be true of more and more people. However there are still large sections of the population whose lives radically exclude books. The intellectually self-conscious, for all their sensitivity and imagination, probably cannot do justice to such people. To lump them (and others) together under the name of the masses is a loss, not a gain in clarity. Following Jean Ethier-Blais it is best—if disheartening—to think of "the mass" as ourselves considered under the aspect of our inertia. As we seek to be taken care of rather than to care, to be certain rather than to risk, to remain embedded in familiar surroundings rather than to grow into our separate individuality, we forego growth and direction. We become enclosed—in tradition, in the company of others, in institutions. Yet our task here is to see something of the *variety* of enclosures in which Canadians live and of the ways we use to break out of these enclosures. Besides, each of us lives through a series of *divergent* enclosures. Our past and present families, neighbourhoods, and associations represent varied, not uniform constraints.

We simply have to conduct our discussion in the presence of the vivid fact that there are many styles of living in this country. Their relative similarities and differences have yet to be adequately explored. Our work, our choice of wallpaper, our patterns of hospitality, our sense of continuity with the past—these help yield a style of life. Styles of living combine and divide. They help make strangers. If *David and Lisa*, the movie, means much to you and to your neighbour in the dark it is silly enough for him to leave; you will have nothing to say to him in the light. You may wonder whether he, too, might walk away in contempt from "a bunch of screwballs, spoiling the town." But of course you can still talk to him about golf, trout, or hockey. Besides, he may be much more comfortable around adolescents than you are, for all your enthusiasm about *Catcher in the Rye*.

Surely it makes a difference to my sense of what matters and how I matter, whether I drive a bus or mine coal, fish salmon for a living or mend cars, work for the government or run elevators, make suits or heal nerves. We, in this room, or as readers of this book are driven to examine life and to argue about the ideas necessary to examine it. But the inarticulate, even the unexamined life, still has its riches. We have yet to invent the methods to bring these to light: conversation is not often likely to tell us what they are.

In pointing to the limitations of our vision, I do not wish to become romantic. No one is free from conflict. No enduring social pattern fails to exact a price. If we want private property, we shall have to like walls and be prepared to encounter thieves. If we cherish our children and the chance to be fully responsible for them when they are very young, we shall, indeed, have to live within certain routines and be able to provide for them in reliable ways even when as parents we would often rather be footloose and fancy free. If we want to pursue the truth, we may have to turn our back on the past and cut some of our roots. If we want rising standards of living, we must develop a complex division of labour and an industrial technology. If we want peace, we have to create rules which make negotiation and trust possible. Our social life, then, is conditional. This fact is thoroughly apparent. Yet the actual extent and intensity of delight and suffering found among us remain hidden. No one knows precisely what price we pay for what. "Most men," said Thoreau, "lead lives of quiet desperation." But how true is this? And if we are uncertain about the volume of distress lining our collective experience, we are even more in the dark about the extent of delight. Delight is very hard to assess. Our methods, in these matters, are biased toward fear and pain. Nor, in the face of crisis, can we be too sure about the strengths of our commitments. Finally, it is also apparent that we always live in more than one realm. To an extent we want what we have. Unless there were some coincidence between the facts and our desires we could not persist. But the coincidence is far from complete. We want more—and less—than we have. We also want what we have never had and to be free from what we know. We cannot live only with regard to what is so. We live also in a realm of possibilities, of phantasies, of wishes.

The Garden of Eden, I dare say, is one sample of the realm of our wishes. There appearance coincides with reality, for Adam and Eve are naked. What is so is also apparent. There is company, but not a crowd. There are conversations but no quarrels. Adam and Eve have no worries: they are well taken care of. Nor are they obliged to work to earn their keep. They are kept, provided they keep some rules. But that is another matter. Their freedom does not at first undo them. They do not fall apart in the absence of a challenge. They tend the garden and enjoy it. They live where they are active and are spared a journey to work. Yet even this wishful realm is conditional. It can be taken away when a special and persistent wish—the wish to explore, even at the risk of disobedience—leads them on. Characteristically enough, they are tempted. Temptations light up the fact that we cannot simply live in a single realm—however much we may say that we wish we could. Adam, presumably, preferred novelty to obedience. He may even have desired to do wrong, at the cost of punishment, for the sake of exploring his own strength and the character of authority. Perhaps all genuine novelty, whether it be in the form of knowledge or new institutions, involves such rebellion, such conflict.

I would claim, however, that the genuine conflict between my desires as well as my convictions of goodness, on the one hand, and the dictates of others, of tradition or of authority, on the other hand, is the place to *end* rather than to *begin* a dissection of the conflicts in the social sphere.

That sphere has a constitution. The social sphere consists of our relations to one another. Friends, clients, children, citizens—these and many others involve the fact of our relatedness. Our relatedness is an open fact. It can be friendly or inimical, public or private, closed to new additions or welcoming them. Whatever the kind of relation we may have in mind, any social relation involves interpretations of the past and expectations of the future. Of necessity, social relations—when thought through—raise questions of inclusion and exclusion: certain expressions, in the form of feelings, thoughts, and facts, are appropriate; others are not. To be a father to my children is not to treat them as employees or friends or clients, but as my *children* and as *my* (or, as you might object, *our*) children. My relation to them actually proceeds in the company of several "orders." As I play ball with my son, we participate in four realms. We participate in the realm of culture, a realm of ideas and values. In contrast to certain other spheres—say the economic one—the realm of ideas and values has the property of being divisible without loss. Shakespeare is not diminished by being read by many rather than few. In order to play with my son we must come to share certain general ideas, about time and space, about fairness and flexibility, about victory and defeat. Thus the game can proceed and what we do can be called a game. As such it can be distinguished from other things we do. Later I shall have to say to him that eating is not a game and that the utensils for salt and pepper cannot do—until later still—as the beginnings of a goods train. The social sphere, then, requires general ideas and ideals. It demands, further, that these be embedded in the partly repetitive, partly changing back-and-forth which binds people. This back-and-forth, creating bonds, is the second realm: it is the social realm proper. It is a realm of relations, of exchange between individuals.

The social realm always exists "between" the realm of ideas and ideals and two other realms: the realm of myself (and my life cycle) and the realm of my body, of nature in general. By the realm of myself, I mean just that: I, though never wholly without others, in becoming myself, am different from all others. Ask me who I am and I shall have to tell you, at least in part, with whom I belong and who are my strangers. But I am also embodied. I am an example of the natural order. I age. The structure of my body, including its early helplessness, demands others and their institutions if my body is to yield its capacities. In turn society receives its shape in part from physical facts: from the faces of its members, from the fact that we have two eyes and not four, a front and a back, definite and limited senses. Age and sex, given by nature and elaborated by man, are among the grounds of our ultimate conflict.

Social relations, then, are built of expectations. In part these expectations grow out of our general sense of what is appropriate; in part they grow out of our changing interpretations of the past. Expectations help define the future. They move us on. They help constitute our bonds. Our bonds, loose or tight, represent mixtures of contrary elements. All bonds include and exclude. Within the changing web of bonds we become ourselves. In becoming ourselves we exchange coherence with another body for a self-contained coherence. The degree and character of our self-containedness vary considerably. Some exchange the body of a mother for the walls of an institution. Some leave their embeddedness and fasten on autonomy. Some use their autonomy to further the autonomy of others; others seek for asymmetry, remaining alone but binding others to themselves. The self, whatever its form, comes to stand against some, if not many, others with whom either it cannot be at ease or be itself or whom it finds alien. None of us escapes the confrontation with others who, for all their physical proximity, seem part of a distant "them." Their distance is expressed in expectations which we cannot share. Yet the experience of closeness and distance obscures the fact that others are a necessary condition for our individuality.

The self, for all its aloneness, is a social gift. No one of us had the freedom to refuse our conception. Though all of us can disown the past, none of us would be here without the care of others. The quality of that care is another matter. If then we experience society as an enemy, because it constrains, we are intellectually only half right. Our constrained desires owe their origins, at least in part, to the ways in which from the beginning we were always both insiders and outsiders. If we want to be free, yet believe others (society) will not allow us to be free, our very wish is engendered by our social experience. Our experience requires others, just as our freedom demands their assent or submission. It is almost as though the social realm is constitutionally divided against itself, just as the self can speak *and* listen—and do both alone. The character of our opposition to society, in other words, itself derives from society. The vitality or fitfulness of our opposition on the other hand may be a matter of temperament, or of some other natural quality. If I value reason or hope or autonomy in opposition to a prevailing commitment to feeling, despair, and mutual support, that very opposition helps to give body to my values.

The very structure of social relations, then, involves a reciprocity between us, be we enemies, friends, clients, or acquaintances, which is always dependent on differences and agreement, on stubborn givens of time and place and on choices including some virtues and excluding others. To me moral conflict—the incompatible demands upon the same person of virtues simultaneously appropriate or the conflicting commitments of persons who must or wish to act in concert—can only be understood within a context wider than the realm of ideas and ideals. I seek to understand individuals and the patterns of living they sustain or bequeath to others.

What particular virtues, for example, would collide in our dealings with one another? Glibly put, one would immediately think of the conflict between equality and inequality. It haunts us. We scoff at notions of equality which are too simple, for we know that some must have more power than others; some must care, and some be cared for; some are bright and some dull. But give a man and a woman also a chance. Let ability count. Let origins not wholly limit the future. Let there be mobility. But honour goes unequally to different lines of work. Still, let each man's vote count the same. It is easy to go on. It is hard to explain the resultant pattern to a child. It is clear that our resolution of the conflict is at best uneasy. It is also true that there has been much change. Access to education has been widened. Education, in turn, becomes increasingly the condition of entering an occupation. Occupation helps bestow and withhold our privileges.

As a moral conflict, equality lives in the company of others. We believe in expanding the scope of reason, in reaching high levels of detachment. We also seek intense attachments free from the calculation of the market-place. At least the calculations should not be first considerations. We value spontaneity, but also seek responsible conduct. We reward loyalty, but we would have a man cut his ties for the sake of a career. Can one really decline a better job for the sake of staying near one's friends? We put people forever in the middle between circles they should leave and circles they cannot yet enter. We depend on the services of the professions only to find that as clients we must learn a delicate balance of trust and distance in order to benefit from the "detached concern" of those who are paid to have our interest at heart.[1]

Even these sporadic examples show that our conflicts require a wider setting for their understanding. They show, too, that our conflicts are of different kinds. All of them probably hurt. But do they all hinder? Do not misunderstand: I am not accepting as necessary what is so. I do refuse to equate conflict with disorganization, or the discussion of values with moral decline.

What would this wider setting be? It seems we can speak of industrial societies, of which Canada as well as Japan and Russia are examples. Such societies share a very widely and deeply distributed commitment to the mastery of the world, both the external world of nature and the internal world of social institutions. Such mastery thrives on knowledge and demands the cultivation of it. With knowledge comes self-consciousness. One of the fruits of this self-consciousness has been the charting of our labyrinthine desires. Ironically these are becoming known to us as we are elaborating the more impersonal patterns of bureaucratic organizations. Such organizations, in turn, are one aspect of the cumulative differentiation of our division of labour. The complexity of our division of labour, in turn, is part and parcel of the greater internal variety of society as such. In principle, if not in practice, there are many circles in which one can move, many styles of life which one can consider. This diversity, in our case, is surely one aspect of our commitment to certain individual freedoms. It may be true that "der Freiheit letzter Sieg wird trocken

---

[1] Merton, W. E., "Sociological Ambivalence," in E. A. Tiryakian (ed.), *Sociological Theory, Values and Sociological Change: Essays in Honour of Pitirim A. Sorokin*, N.Y., The Free Press, 1963.

sein"—that for all our advance in the length of life and in general standards of living we are in fact moving toward a dry security with sporadic withdrawals into various emotional interludes; but it may also be true that we shall become free to be leisurely. This leisure, by the way, we probably did not really quite intend to create. It was perhaps a by-product of our efficiency.

Our virtues precede *and* follow what we do. Their wider context, then, is governed by the general demand for mastery. This demand leaves things wide open. In the case of Canada it lives with notions of freedom. To an extent one is free to live without the drive for achievement. One can participate in quite different ways in the same society, still claiming allegiance to the same virtues. These further include our commitments to the notions of justice, of social variety, of individual health and security.

What kinds of moral conflict within the relations among its members does such a society make possible? There is, first, the incongruity among values as such. For all our commitments to mastery, we also preach acceptance. For all our belief in merit and impersonal considerations, we also cherish personal obligations. *In fact, it is the conflict between the personal and the impersonal which perhaps causes more tensions than any other within our social relations.* Apparently one of our major concerns is with individual independence, with initiative, with standing on one's own feet. Yet our yearnings go toward attachment, to being close to something, true to something. While we limit our involvements and often keep ourselves anonymous, or only partly disclosed, we also want to be understood, to be comprehended. We want the efficiency that comes from treating people as numbers. We want to reward competence and judge it fairly, *sine ira et studio*. We want positive knowledge as widely and deeply as possible, yielding assertions which do not depend on personal experience. We want mobility and the right to be accepted on the basis of our specific merits rather than as members of families. Often we want to be treated as though we had no past. Often, too, the other person matters only as a means: he fills the car with gas, she serves us meals on a plane. Many of our relations seek an impersonal mode—in the names of justice, efficiency, achievement, privacy, or rational mastery. This impersonality is not of a piece. Teachers and telephone operators must remain detached from those they serve, but the teacher's detachment accompanies concern. It also accompanies daily encounters with children who are emotionally fully there. Yet for all our commitments to impersonality, we prize as well those who care, especially if they care for ourselves in our own right. We may even hope that they care unconditionally, and so suspend the constitution of the social realm. It is probably no accident that the same society should cultivate impersonal achievement and intense, personal love.

There are other incongruities of a similar kind. These I can only list. We seek equality, at least within limits; but we also wish to make room for excellence. We want freedom, including the freedom to go as far as we can with our gifts or our resources; but we also want to keep narrow the gap between rich and poor. We believe in the common man and maintain a series of elites.

We can all participate in these incongruities. Some then seek to escape into a permanent resolution; others move from temporary solutions to new impasses, finding the journey itself worth the price of its pain.

There are, secondly, incongruities which befall us by virtue of the fact that we are bounded by age and sex. To be a woman, in our society, is to suffer conflicting demands and opportunities. These play about the contrast between attachment and achievement, between the cultivation of beauty and care and the right to limit one's involvement in the name of transcending any one type of social relation, be it that of wife or mother or daughter. This is not the place to determine whether women suffer more conflicts than men, or suffer more from the conflicts which they, and men, receive or create from one another. Needless to say the capacities and limitations of the sexes are also embedded in the contrasts and changes between the generations.

Thirdly, we have asked of some—scientists in industry, intellectuals in government, even professors in universities—to live simultaneously by the special standards of otherwise separate circles. Clearly we would have far more conflict, if in our society our general virtues were not in the form of many special codes which become the characteristic privileges of different categories or circles of individuals. Further, whatever conflict I may suffer from the demands of work and home, work itself yields divergent demands: to teach, to enquire and write, to be politically responsible within the university community—these compete for one's time. More than that, they require contrary attitudes. Scholars should be modest. Reformers cannot hide their light under a bushel. As a student one must see many sides; as a citizen of our academic community one must choose one side or another.

Further still, there are the special conflicts closely linked to the antinomies of our life cycle which arise whenever we care for another. If we were to analyse in some detail the relations between professional persons and their clients, between parents and children, between teachers and students, we would lay bare a delicate pattern of balances among opposites. Why else would we speak about art in these matters?

Let me mention two other kinds of conflict: conflicts within the self and the contradiction between "content" and "form." We wrestle in various ways, probably throughout our lives, with various modes of autonomy and attachment. We experiment, at times giving up one for the sake of enhancing the other. We may be irked by this dialogue for it can paralyse. In the end, I suspect we must live with it, if we wish to be alive. The enclosures, which we need, in other words, are never enough. The self must ultimately die alone.

As for the contradiction between "content" and "form" it also cannot be dissolved without doing away with the fullness of things. Our social encounters proceed in a "severalness": whenever we say something, our manner of saying it adds to our expression a further dimension which can qualify and even undo what we said. Let me illustrate:

> A young man who had fairly well recovered from an acute schizophrenic episode was visited in the hospital by his mother. He was glad to see her and impulsively put his arm around her shoulder, whereupon she stiffened. He withdrew his arm and she asked, "Don't you love me any more?" He then blushed, and she said, "Dear, you must not be so easily embarrassed and afraid of your feelings." The patient was able to stay with her only a few minutes more and following her departure he assaulted an aide and was put in the tubs.
>
> Obviously, this result could have been avoided if the young man had been able to say, "Mother, it is obvious that you have difficulty accepting a gesture of affection from me." However, the schizophrenic patient doesn't have this possibility open to him. His intense dependency and training prevents him from commenting upon his mother's communicative behaviour, though she comments on his and forces him to accept and to attempt to deal with the complicated sequence.[2]

Finally, of course, many of our social encounters involve the conflicts of bargains and of interests. Such conflicts are contained by our virtues. We should remember them because they remind us that in our encounters we move away from bargains or toward them—but we probably seldom leave them behind. Similarly we move toward or away from generosity and trust. Yet even in the coolest of calculations affecting another, we cannot ultimately succeed in treating him as a mere means.

Competitors must trust each other and abide by rules which ensure the continuity of competitions. Even husbands and wives include in their relations economic and legal arrangements which would limit the free

[2]Bateson, G. *et al.*, "Toward a Theory of Schizophrenia," *Behavioral Science*, 1.4 (October 1956): 251-64.

play of sheer trust and spontaneity. Some impersonality is the condition of persistence. Some faith is the condition of economic exchange. This continuity among contrary elements, which, through their different proportions, constitute the difference among our relations, allows for the kind of shock which enlightens us. Virtue can be feigned. Trust can be misused. Intimacy can be turned into a bargain. Bargains can be presented as personal favours. There is, in fact, no way of ensuring the quality, intensity, and continuity of our commitments or of those with whom we wish to sustain a bond. As a result no society is completely free to refrain from using some form of fear—and its derivatives of guilt and shame—in order to provide for the exclusion of inappropriateness on too large a scale. Yet complete domination is impossible. Complete destruction, of course, *is* possible. Short of both, the necessity of virtue for the persistence of individuality introduces into all our relations the permanent fact of risk and uncertainty, of surprise and disappointment, of waxing and waning in our commitments. Would it not naturally follow from this that some conflict is to be welcomed? Perfect ordering would surely spell death.

What of the causes of conflict in the social sphere? These strike me:

1. We hold out ideas of success throughout our society but we do not provide the opportunities for achieving such success equally uniformly. This disproportion between ends and means, as Merton has shown,[3] invites disaffection. Some of us withdraw, sometimes quietly build a counter-world, cultivate our gardens or, in the extreme, confront the world as hobos or schizophrenics. Some rebel, wishing to undo or redo this world, often in the name of virtues or intensities which our adult compromises otherwise forestall. Some lead the lives of hollow men who only work here. They want to be asked no questions. They do not believe in what they are doing. They go through the motions. They support families. They attend functions. Yet they have given up. Sometimes they are ready to march if someone leads them. Some cling to the virtues but seek new ways since ordinary ones appear closed. They steal or commit crimes. Ironically they confirm the form of society while evading some of its rules. The social sphere thus becomes a criss-cross of commitments and counter-commitments. It creates insiders and outsiders who frequently depend on each other. It creates the endless ambiguity of public disapproval and private admiration and the endless argument over punishment and cure. Vice, finally, provides careers on both of its sides—for those who wish to contain and replace it and for those who

[3]Merton, R. K., "Social Structure and Anomie," in *Social Theory and Social Structure*, Glencoe, Ill., The Free Press, 1961.

wish to follow it. Nor do we doubt that this will cease. Some of us believe, though, that enlarging the notion of achievement, and even more the opportunity to accomplish it, will lessen the likelihood of disaffection.

2. We tend to balance our demand for impersonality and independence by creating opportunities, mostly within the sphere of kinship and friendship, for personal fullness and immediacy. Thus we live in an uneven world, forever crossing boundaries. The coherence thereby lost may be made up for by the variety gained. But this horizontal balance, complementing our occupational rationality with domestic irrationality, crosses a vertical discontinuity between the large reservoir of dependence enclosed by our childhood and the independence demanded of us as adults.

3. Canadian society restricts enthusiasm. A bald statement, worth disproving. But is this culture not muted? Yes, you may agree—but not in French Canada. The contrast would illustrate my point. Intensity is suspect. It reminds one of adolescence. If we must choose we are urged to be Apollonian, not Dionysian—even at the risk of ending with human forms that have some of the qualities of plastic. This way we are not just to ourselves. One feels surrounded and inhabited by much unlived life. To be sure we differ in our temperaments. There are probably many who are quietly pleased to be alive. Nor am I arguing for general shouting and noise-making. But the inhibition of our emotions—and hence, admittedly, the avoidance of pain—provides one often with the chance to look into a face which seems more burdened than alive.

4. We talk much about sincerity, identity, integrity. Such talk seems like a desperate gesture at times. It cannot undo the tide of endless public persuasion, of fake enthusiasm by paid sellers of new products. The gesture arises from the fact of the huge variety of our social world. But such variety must in the end still be met by an individual inner coherence—or else we are nothing. The demand for coherence, however, has to accommodate itself to a demand for flexibility, for participation even within a short time-span, and not just in a lifetime, in social arrangements which are very different from one another. Discontinuity and contrast are both valued and irksome facts. Response to contrast is also valued. To weep with those that weep and to laugh with those that laugh is not hypocrisy or even "other-orientation." In our society, moreover, we have to sustain our moods of joy and grief in close proximity to others whose moods are radically different. A city is full of incompatible events within a small space. The virtues of fidelity and honesty and of compassion and concern have no easy time of it.

5. I trust you do not think it is anti-intellectual if I point to knowledge as another source of strain. As a means of our mastery, knowledge has

also become a source of our sense of being flooded. The virtue of individuality and hence of uniqueness confronts the fact that individually we are also generally quite replaceable, quite small. Bodies of knowledge, organizations, webs of people—these make the difference. But it is not so much knowledge considered as a form of flood surrounding us that is a source of conflict. Rather, knowledge and the self-consciousness it yields (as well as the manipulation) fight with spontaneity. The truth, moreover, may make us free—but it can surely make us sad. Yet to forego the search for more answers and new questions is impossible. Our minds go limp if they do not move on; they hallucinate if they cannot confront a changing outer world. The solvent for this conflict may lie in humour. Indeed, the existence of humour is both proof of our state of conflict and the means of transforming it productively.

6. Finally, in this haphazard listing of the causes which supply the social world with its conflicts, let me suggest the problem of mutual confirmation. We may scoff at the wish for approval, but in isolation human nature decays. Genuine commitments to the virtues involves their meaningful experience with others whose similar commitments help provide support and who can understand, and so accept, the discrepancy between wish and fact. Their understanding in turn makes possible one's declarations. For this there must be time and continuity. I suspect we go short in both respects. Understanding, moreover, proceeds on the back of shared memories and allows for many short cuts. It encompasses the undercurrent of our unsaid thoughts and gives them a fair place and chance.

Strains such as these demand their solution. We can be radical and turn our back on this world. But we cannot do so absolutely. The celibate life, for instance, dissolves many conflicts and allows for a concentration for which the rest of us are not free. But were it not for the rest of us there would soon be no candidates for celibacy. One can seek a fundamentalist reaction, dissolving the risk and ambiguity of social life within the confines of a closed ideology or leaving it behind within emotion and trance. One can succumb to apathy. One can court kicks. One can just waste, weary with the pervasive ugliness of the endless chain of second-hand car lots, dog hospitals, funeral parlors, and drive-in cafes which introduce us to our cities. One can spin webs of suspicion or establish secure routines. Most of us, I imagine, oscillate between necessary compromises and sporadic visions of the possibilities for change and the actual extent of goodness and imagination which still give the constructive forces a much greater chance than the destructive ones. Not all conflict paralyses. Some conflict is the very expression of our freedom.

Some is the opportunity of private or recognized heroism. Genuine coherence, be it of ourselves or between us and others, surely requires for its growth the opportunity of taming conflicts. But the conflicts that hinder our growth could be reduced. This is a matter of ordering our social institutions so that they would have more room for honesty, and for aliveness. As a society that is still open we have the chance to do this —especially if we add to our efforts to create social and individual security the genuine encouragement of seeing many things, even familiar ones, as though for the first time.

SOCIAL INJUSTICE AND RATIONAL REFORM

THOMAS BALOGH

I wish to discuss those problems of psychological unbalance and conflict of values which are caused by the structure and functioning of our social system and which could, therefore, be dealt with by rational reform. I shall leave the problem of individual spiritual anguish to be resolved by the individual.

Professor Galbraith has analysed the tendency to social unbalance with both penetration and unsurpassed wit. The rise in national income, he shows, will not bring with it unquestioned satisfaction if it is stimulated mainly by the artificial creation of new needs rather than a balanced advance over a broad social front. "Psychological obsolescence" creates a sense of increasing frustration when general needs are neglected. A tendency toward greater inequality, toward a *relative* reduction in consumption, and an increase in conspicuous waste create their own undoing in terms of happiness. The increase in production, instead of resulting in increased leisure, increased education, and increased general amenity, without which leisure cannot be enjoyed, is concentrated on creating new individual material needs, creating discontent in order that the supply of these needs may provide outlets for new enterprise. Collective needs, because they demand collective resources, are discouraged, and intense propaganda is waged against "molly-coddling" through better schools, hospitals, libraries, whose support demands high tax-revenue.

Domestic social tension must inevitably be generated in two directions by the process of affluent growth. On the one hand, stability without controls implies a threat to, if not actual loss of, the livelihood of a growing majority. On the other hand, collective wants are disregarded, while at the same time conspicuous consumption has to be artificially stimulated. A feeling of growing spiritual poverty and dissatisfaction as well as guilt, impatience, and aggression are inevitable in the long run in such a society.

In his analysis of the problem of the "affluent society," Professor Galbraith lays much emphasis not merely on the inherent tendency to a basic misuse of resources and the neglect of urgent collective wants, but also on the paramount position of production, which, in his view, is due to irrational adherence to "conventional wisdom." The ever-insistent "concern for production" is a result of the economics of scarcity: "The ancient preoccupations of economic life—with equality, security and productivity—have now narrowed down to a preoccupation with productivity and production." "Production," he says, "has become the solvent of tensions. . . ." He goes on to propose indirect taxation to deal with social unbalance, and suggests that preoccupation with production could be eliminated through greatly increased unemployment benefits. Once leisure and good income can be vouchsafed, there is no more need to press for higher production. Here is a brilliantly simple suggestion for the solution of the contemporary psychological problem.

In fact it is too simple a solution. It might be superficially correct to say that everybody seems concerned with higher production when, in fact, we do not need it. But this concern is neither universal nor does it on close inspection go very deep. It is not merely the employment and income of the many which is at stake. The creation of wants and dissatisfaction is not merely an indirect Calvinist way of providing work to minimize unemployment. It is an inevitable consequence of the paramountcy of profits, which is at the centre of the system. Inasmuch as Professor Galbraith's proposals would leave profits severely menaced, they are doomed to failure in our society, just as Keynes was doomed to failure when he exhorted the bankers of the world to "save themselves" —when they, in fact, were making sure that their dominance would continue—at the cost of harsh and inevitable losses.

Each individual firm, however large, still has its own problems and risks to face. These risks, no doubt, are far less than when all or at least most firms were small and faced with an overwhelming and unmanageable impersonal market. The immense casualty rate of small businesses in America and Britain gives an impression of the sort of risks that were faced, though, of course, they are influenced by the fact that the smallest businesses are now in the retail trade or building, which have peculiar problems. But the risk is there and it is only diminished by purposeful action, which weakens the only feature of an individualist economy that is claimed to establish the superiority of the system over a centrally planned one. There is no longer an impersonal market giving unmistakable and absolute direction to entrepreneurs who have no choice at all.

The feverish drive to manipulate consumer demand, product differentiation and fragmentation into different types, the reluctance to embark on too rapid an expansion, especially in the basic industries in which demand is more unstable—all these characteristics of a mature economy based on mass-consumption render that economy less capable of matching the performance of centrally planned systems. Conversely, they represent the new guise of the age-old problem of an economy based on private ownership and production for profit in contrast to need. So long as there is no means by which losses can be equalized, or rather borne by the community, it is difficult, if not impossible, to prohibit measures which reduce risks and increase profit unless there are socially directly noxious, as, for example, the sale of dangerous drugs. There are a host of other practices which are perhaps more damaging to social integration or to individual satisfaction and human progress than medically dangerous drugs. The deliberate creation of dissatisfaction, the stimulus to status-seeking through conspicuous consumption, the incitement to social difference working on the knowledge which modern psychology has unearthed, the playing on the sense of insecurity to encourage people to identify themselves with groups outwardly full of goodwill but fiercely competitive in reality, the use of human frailty for profit-making purposes when concentrated education and psycho-therapy are needed to mitigate it—all this seems inevitable in a system of fragmented risk-bearing.

Only better education, a government-financed counter-propaganda, and a purposeful direction of both could introduce balance. But how can there be organized purposeful education? Government pursuasion, it is agreed, might mean brain-washing. Thus the liberal philosopher pleads for a plurality of cultures, which should co-exist peacefully side by side. The argument for non-interference is as skilled as it is spurious.

A common culture, it is said, would have to be imposed, and if it has to be imposed it cannot satisfy. Has modern psychology not triumphantly demonstrated that only a freely accepted way of life and system of wants would really be satisfying?

The liberalised society is one where men fulfil themselves according to their own view or conception of life—provided, of course, that in doing so they do not interfere with, or upon, the self-fulfilment of others. To achieve this they must be free both of the dictates of established authority and of the subtler but no less effective power of social pressure. Furthermore, they must have free access to the principal ideas evolved in the course of human history concerning the conduct of life. . . .[1]

All this sounds rather wonderful and noble. It is said that Oxford philosophers nowadays specialize in the meaning of language in order to solve difficult questions which have eluded their predecessors because they were not correctly formulated. If this be so, this passage certainly does not exemplify it—unless it is to be taken as a rather emotional affirmation of the author, by the use of general "hurray words," of his preference for a negative-libertarian state in which he who has had a certain culture very forcefully drummed into him can fulfil himself according to his—formidable—lights. How is one to interpret, for instance, the formula that "men should fulfil themselves according to their own view or conception of life," when the question is that of mass-conditioning of largely defenceless consumers, with all the power of modern psychology by large and powerful vested interests? The problem in the modern non-Soviet state is no longer the abuse of superior dragooning power by its sole monopolist possessor, the state, but the contrast between the unorganized, unskilled, unadvised mass of consumers existing in small family units, without, in the main, any call on expenditure, and the vast array of power unaccountable in any direct way to anyone. How can one say that "men" should be free "of the dictates of established authority," meaning the state, or even of "subtler but no less effective social pressures," unless one can envisage a far-reaching control of the economic power which is behind a large number of these pressures, through advertising or the private ownership of the means of communication? The implication that the sole thing to be done to set people free is to abolish censorship and the political police, is surely misleading in the extreme.

Nor is the problem of education, of enabling people to have "free access to the principal ideas evolved in the course of human history," handled either with discernment or with complete candour. It is easy to talk about free access to the principal ideas which have animated human history. Is it to be understood that this is feasible without a complete transformation of mass-education? Mr. Wollheim rightly stresses the need for a largely increased educational effort to give some semblance of substance to the claim of "equality of opportunity." But what *is* education but compulsion? It is the object of every totalitarian regime to "set the people free" to be able "freely" to accept the dominant doctrine of the regime. It is interesting to observe that those authors who are among the most libertarian are those who have been subjected to the most thorough

[1] Richard Wollheim, *Socialism and Culture*, Fabian Tract, 331, p. 47.

intellectual conditioning (they would call it dragooning and brainwashing if done to others by other institutions) which can be experienced outside the most stringent Communist elite schools of propaganda or the Roman Catholic Church—the English Public School system following a Preparatory School, and followed in its turn by Oxbridge.[2] It is odd that they should protest against a more widespread educational venture or less totalitarian lines as being "imposed." While strenuously protesting their advanced thinking, they seem to have fallen victim to rather simple eighteenth-century rationalist notions on human nature.

Modern psychology has shown that dragooning and conditioning take place from the day of birth; some more extreme psychoanalysts hold that it possibly begins antenatally. The original instincts have to be tamed and modified. The individual, in his formative years, consciously and unconsciously absorbs a vast array of notions and prohibitions. His reactions will vary. But to talk as if the "men"—except for a very small, privileged, and rich class—would or could possibly live their lives "according to their *own* view or conception of life" in a modern community, exposed as they are to the social pressures and the need to earn a living, to say that they can have by themselves "free access" to the principal ideas of humanity without education is rather misleading. The collective word "men" simply hides the problem of the plurality of cultures in the non-Soviet world. Here mass-culture is provided on an entirely different basis, and with a purpose different from that of the minority culture received for the few. Without education, "men" cannot absorb ideas and form them into their own conceptions. They are provided with a conception. Education itself may be the inculcation of a set of moral and aesthetic values determined by contemporary society. And here is the rub—the eternal dilemma of the liberal reformer. Because education is compulsion, a reform of the traditional culture climate necessarily demands counter-compulsion. The reformer who does not accept the dilemma but averts his eyes by pleading non-intervention, on the plea of preserving liberty, merely favours the compulsion implicit in the *status quo* with its open and hidden persuasions.

If this is the case in rich industrialized areas, the fate of under-developed territories is far worse when it comes to applying our techniques and values to their problems. Here the mechanical transposition of Western values has led to an extraordinary perversion of intent. I shall take as an illustration the problem of education in Africa with

---

[2] It has been perhaps one of the most successful and completely deliberate totalitarian education experiments ever witnessed, bringing forth a monolithic ruling-class for the Victorian Empire.

which I have been connected in the last few years and where I am fighting a desperate rearguard action against people of the utmost goodwill animated by the most noble desires.

An essential requirement of educational reform is re-orientation toward agricultural progress. This has been conspicuously absent in African educational movements and it must be said that the achievement of independence has, on the whole, meant no change at all. It is not difficult to explain the origins of the grave, indeed the gravest, problem which Africans now face. It reaches back into the past history of the newly independent countries. The attitude to education of their population, broad masses and elite alike, is determined by their previous experience, which has little, if any, relevance to the problems of the future. The educational system is necessarily an adjunct of the society and the state organization in which it arises. Until recently, the framework and functioning of African government, both on the local and on the higher level, were determined by the principle of maintaining law and order and providing the structure for the economic activity of large expatriate private firms and individuals and for an unchanging subsistence agriculture in the traditional sector.

The machinery of the state and of education was thus geared to assure a minimum requirement for this purpose and no more. In the French territories, the aim was to assure educational equality at each stage with the corresponding institutions of the Metropolis. The schools in the periphery were exact replicas of analogous institutions in France, and it can be asserted with some force that their particular aims, very elevated perhaps but certainly wholly irrelevant for the future prosperity of Africa, were successfully achieved. In the British territory, too, the educational system was modelled after the British. Voluntary mission schools were complemented by private secondary schools and some pre-college education was provided and subsequently expanded; after the war, university colleges, closely modelled on Oxford and Cambridge, completed the picture.

The accent on quality, of which this system of education was an expression, must not be dismissed. It had its advantages. But from the viewpoint of the emergent African states, this system necessarily constituted a hindrance rather than a help. The scarcity of educational facilities, and the consequent restriction of entry to the children of the influential and less poor, gave it an aristocratic slant not unlike that in Britain of the pre-Victorian Reform era. Consequently, education, far from providing the economy with better-trained manpower at every stage and level, was increasingly considered incompatible with menial jobs, that is, any kind of job involving manual labour and more especially agricultural labour. As a result, even the most rudimentary relationship with education threatens to alienate its beneficiary both from the milieu in which he has been brought up and the improvement which ought really to be the essential aim of the educational process.

This extremely anti-social and anti-progressive impact of education has been much accentuated, paradoxically enough, by the quest for equality by Africans interpreted in a peculiar and, it must be said, destructive sense. The representatives of the colonial powers, for reasons which are historically comprehensible, had been educated in this "general" fashion. And, in the historical context, this was right. What was required by the colonial governments and the large metropolitan corporations was ability to manage affairs, ability to administer both states and great corporations which hired technical experts when required. Thus the population of the African states which such administrators governed became conscious of the great advantage in terms of personal careers of a general arts education. The fact that administrators came from well-connected families enhanced this impression. The strong differentiations of the African social structure predisposed the acceptance and perpetuation of such attitudes. The prestige of this non-technical education rose with the examples of success which it achieved in all the territories of Africa. The Sorbonne and the arts faculties of the ancient universities of England contributed equally, each in its way, to the crystallization of this attitude. In practically all countries, this attitude also involved a disparagement of the importance and status of technical knowledge. Vocational training was looked down upon. In the hierarchical structure of Africa, technical and educational services were placed well below the (well-connected) general administrator. This stratification, inimical to social and economic progress, has not changed with independence. The formidable social obstacles and vested interests in the way of such a change have been reinforced by the process of the so-called Africanization of the government services, which accepted as valid equality of status with that of the foreign administrators. Not only was the differentiation between administrators and technical experts perpetuated, but also that between the government services and the mass of the people.

The spread of education built on this basis is wrong for Africa because its essential characteristic is that of elite education of a type which presupposes a large uneducated mass doing menial jobs. In addition, the cost would be crushing to the Africans. In sum, the quest for equality between the new national and the old metropolitan elite of colonial days has destroyed equality altogether within Africa. We have perpetuated, as a result of the imposition of equality and of quality education into a system which it does not fit, an inequality and a frozen productive structure which will certainly make it almost impossible to create a modern and happy life in these African states.

If Africa is to be provided with the manpower needed for modern administration of a fast-expanding economy promising higher standards of life, the status of various careers has to be changed and the inequality of income between the educated and the mass of the people has to be resolutely reduced. Above all, teaching will have to achieve a much higher status, and equality among the Africans themselves will have to be assured.

The problem of education in Africa today illustrates only too clearly how an unthinking quest for the application of certain basic values could pervert the whole progress of a nation.

SCRIPTURAL FAITH AND CULTURAL VALUES

GREGORY BAUM

Since the topic of the origin and development of values in human civilization is intimately connected with the reflection on human history, it is of special concern to the theologian. For it is only through biblical faith that history has become the object of reflection. Only through biblical faith did history tell a meaningful story, one which man had to listen to in order to understand himself. In non-biblical cultures, the man of wisdom sought to penetrate the contingent, and hence the historical, to discover the lasting and necessary behind the shifting scene of events; the movement of wisdom constantly transcended historical existence to eternal verities. To be in history was really a pity. Opinion, and not science, was the kind of knowledge that could be drawn from man's historical existence.

This lack of appreciation of history is not surprising, since it was impossible for the ancient philosophers to give a meaningful interpretation of historical events. A philosopher may enlarge his view, he may take in long stretches of time and vast areas of human culture, but he is never certain whether this circle has encompassed all that is significant. Since he constantly suspects that what he studies is only a section of human culture, he will not dare to discuss its orientation. In such a case, meaning is not in history, but in being saved from history. In order to say anything significant about history and its movement, we must have a point transcending history from which to judge it. We must know the beginning and the end of the historical process, or at least know that it has a beginning and an end. For this reason it was the revelation of God in Israel that enabled men to reflect on history.

The revelation of the meaning of history is not incidental to the religion of the Bible; it stands at its very core. There God reveals Himself as the Lord of mercy who has created men in order to join them to Himself in friendship. While men are stubborn and selfish, always breaking the unity of the divine plan, God intervenes in the course of history to form them into a people, *His* people, to redirect their lives to a concern for others, and to liberate them for what is best in themselves. God reveals Himself so that we may know who we are and what is the meaning of our history.

According to the Bible, God is the Lord of history. He directs it as He wishes. At the same time it is man who through his decisions, through the answers he gives to his God, makes history. History is both the locus of divine self-revelation and the creation of man's free decisions. And yet, because even man's freedom is in the hands of the Lord who made him, we know that history will end well: God will see to it that men will be reconciled to Him as His holy people.

From the Judaeo-Christian faith, the conviction that history possesses a destiny, or that historical developments are progressive realizations of a plan, has deeply penetrated Western culture. These ideas have not always entered men's minds through the Church's preaching or through reading the Bible, but whether in line with Christian thought or in opposition to it, the notion of history as having a beginning and a direction, as fulfilling a law and simultaneously as being the locus of human decisions —all this has completely conquered the mind of man. Christianity has taught Western man to be self-conscious about history, not to regard it as an accidental sequence of events, but to study its coherence and interpret its orientation.

The nineteenth-century ideals of evolution and progress were related to biblical faith; but because these theories were created in reaction to conservative religious forces and inspired by humanistic ideals of various kinds, they were basically secularist in outlook, positing a law of development, immanent to history itself. Whether we look at Auguste Comte, who believed that the progress of science would deliver mankind from its enemies and produce a new world, or at Karl Marx, who regarded a necessary sociological dialectic as the inevitable force leading mankind to the perfect society, we are witnessing a faith in history which is nothing but the secularization of Christian hope. Yet if any theory of human progress regards this progress as wholly immanent to humanity itself, it will lose the dimension which has given meaning to history in the first place, namely the free decision of God, and hence will ultimately destroy progress. Thus the Comtean understanding of progress has led to an empty scientism which has closed men's eyes to what is deepest in them and therefore removed the terms in which progress can be measured, and the Marxian ideal of the dialectical progress of history has been usurped as an instrument of power politics and made to serve in the conflict of nations.

Despite these deformations the conviction of history as direction, as progress, remains unchallenged in Western civilization and even the nations of Asia and Africa have caught this spirit from us. They have come to believe in their mission as nations. They now think of themselves as having a contribution to make; they regard our times as "their hour," the propitious moment of their self-realization. History for them is no longer that which is suffered, but that in which they are actively engaged in order to change themselves and modify history.

There may be comparatively few Christians in the world; yet their understanding of history has once and for all caught the minds of men, to be preserved or corrupted, never to be lost. Man has become conscious that he is the master of nature, that he belongs to an order superior to the world that surrounds him, and that he can manipulate the forces of nature by science and technology to serve his own ends. In the great nonbiblical cultures man stood over against nature contemplating its beauty. For them nature gave expression to a cosmic law, to the divine order of things, and man reached his perfection by submitting to the inner harmony of the world of nature. The cosmos was a more perfect image of the divine than was man. In the Scriptures, on the contrary, man is created as the master of creation, destined to know it, to transform it, and to build society. Man, according to the biblical vision, does not submit to the cosmos; while he realizes that his surroundings are largely a given thing which he has not chosen, he is continually called to make decisions which affect his environment and initiate its transformation.

In this limited sense, the world has become Christian. No doubt, this advance remains ambiguous, to be used for good or evil; but the notion of history as destiny has completely transformed our civilization.

The understanding of history as development is related to another value, central in Western civilization, which is derived from biblical revelation, that is, the peculiar dignity of the human person. The men of wisdom of ancient Greece preferred to think of man in terms of his "nature," in terms of what all men have in common, the soul and body, the faculties of intellect and will; and man's involvement in time appeared to them as a contingent or accidental factor. In the Bible, however, man is essentially related to the historical order. It belongs to his essence to be in history. Man is constantly facing a situation which is determined by the past and called upon to enter into a future partially created by his own decision. This freedom of man to transcend the given-ness of each situation by an action which embodies his own decision and transforms his environment is precisely what makes history possible. Animals do not have history. Their lives are determined by impulses. But the essence of man implies the need to decide for himself, and it is only by means of these decisions that he comes to be what he is. Without them he remains a child.

By this freedom (from which God's action in us is not excluded!) we are distinct from the rest of the cosmos, superior to it, belonging to a different order of being. Man is not one object among the many objects of the world; he is a subject, reflecting and making decisions which transform him as well as his surroundings.

This understanding of the human person is of biblical origin; in the Bible we are told that man is created in the image and likeness of God. Man is not an object in the world, but a subject, one who can engage in dialogue with God, the supreme Subject. It is quite true that according to the scriptural account man has lost, through a disloyalty in which the whole race is involved, his freedom and power positively to respond to God, but we are also told that through God's redeeming Word addressed to Israel and finally sent to all men in Jesus Christ, we are set free again to acknowledge God's call and become again, in the true sense, the image of God, the supreme Person.

This understanding of the dignity of the person has profoundly influenced Western thought. Christian and non-Christian thinkers of the West have been overwhelmed by the grandeur of man, despite his failures and his malice. It was especially the Protestant Reformation which brought the realization of the uniqueness of man's freedom to the conscience of the common man, first in Europe and then in America. But here again it is only in a truly Christian context that this personalism does not deteriorate into a self-seeking individualism. The person is not meant to be the centre of his own conscious life. If we set ourselves up as the end of our own personal history, we caricature the order of the world and fall into blinding selfishness. What it means to be a person we are taught profoundly only by God, who addresses us in his Word, and it is in this same Word that we find ourselves belonging to a plan of salvation which embraces the whole people of God. In the Christian message we learn that the dimensions of our freedom are the worship of God and the service of others. We discover ourselves as persons when we love our neighbour.

Despite our hypocrisy, our greed, our injustices, and our crimes, the possibility of progress and the freedom of the human person in love have entered modern human consciousness, probably never to be erased. However much we sin against these insights now, modern civilization is profoundly marked by these Christian values.

When I attribute these values to biblical revelation, I do not wish to belittle the contribution which human thought and the experience of mankind have made to their discoveries. The Christian believes that the Lord of his faith is the Lord of the world and that, therefore, he has not only left an inkling of his plan in the hearts of all men but also, and especially, continues to act in the cultural and religious aspirations of all peoples. While we believe that salvation-history is restricted to Israel and the Christian Church, in the sense that only there do men realize the merciful ways of God with the world, in a wider sense salvation-history pervades the history of all peoples, especially since the coming of Christ. The growing self-realization of man and the unification of the human race, of which we find a beginning in Greek philosophy and many developments in the wisdom of all ages (and more particularly in the aspirations of vast numbers of men in our day) are not unrelated to the initiative of God in the world. Even if men claim that they have discovered these values by reason alone, or by experience or direct intuition, this does not exclude its being the God of history having declared in Christ His universal will to save, who is acting in their spirits. In the understanding of the Christian message, therefore, Christians have always learned from those outside the Church to whom God has given insight, however incomplete.

I wish to stress this point. Declaring that the scriptural faith is the source of cultural values does not mean that from the beginning these values were consciously seized upon by the Christian community. It is rather through the experience of many centuries, when Christians were obliged to put new questions to the Word of God, that much of what this Word contains came to light and produced explicit knowledge. Here are some instances. When America and other lands across the seas were discovered in the sixteenth century, Christians reflected on the gospel in order to find a moral standard applicable to Christians and non-Christians alike. The rise of Marxism in the nineteenth century urged Christians to seek anew in the Christian message the meaning of society and mutual responsibility, and the advance of science and technology have forced Christians to question again God's message regarding the meaning and purpose of the cosmos. The ideas of history as evolution and the human person as unique are derived from the Scriptures, but in the process of their clarification the whole of human experience has been involved, if not with positive insights, then at least with new questions.

I am tempted to go a step further. When the Christian community was blind to values or ideals contained in the gospel, God sent them prophets and saints to remind them; but when the Christian people preferred their comfortable ignorance, God would permit that the yearning for this neglected value would leap beyond the borders of the Church, there to kindle a movement seeking to establish it in society. But because this movement was outside the Church it suffered from the unprotectedness of human life and though its purpose was good, it embraced erroneous ideas, became hostile to the Christian gospel and ultimately initiated its own destruction. Is not most of the post-Christian belief in Western culture, and especially Marxism, a reaction of this kind? Were there not Christian values, neglected in the Church, which caught the hearts of men outside the Church, but in their minds did not these values become secularized and turned against the Church and perhaps even against man? Was not the Enlightenment something which Christians should have carried out? Was not the intention of the French revolution something for which Christians should have worked? Were not the ideals of Marxism aims for which Christians should have laboured? But we were slow to act and God permitted the movement to go on elsewhere, caught up in errors, to become a reproach to us.

As a Roman Catholic, I would extend this interpretation of history by saying that schisms in the Church have been produced in similar ways. Because we did not live up to the ideals of the gospel and heed the prophets sent to the Church, God permitted that these evangelical values stirred men up to begin movements outside the Church and partially against her, standing in judgment over her negligence. And yet these movements of reaction, being unprotected, became subject to distortions and self-destructive tendencies.

The Christian message of selflessness and love contradicts the human inclination on one level. But because the message which God spoke into the world is in harmony *on a deeper level* with human aspirations of which the same God is the author, many, if not most Christians believe that there are certain norms of human behaviour, certain moral ideals, which are common to all human beings whether they are believers or not. The history of human thought testifies to this. The Stoic philosophers spoke of a natural law, and immanent *logos*, to which men must submit to find wisdom and happiness; and the philosophers of the Enlightenment spoke of natural laws of human behaviour, determined by reason, which have universal validity. The formulations of these laws were often at variance, and the grounds for their validity depended on the various systems of philosophy; but they do give witness to the common conviction of mankind that there are common standards of behaviour for all men. Some Protestant thinkers deny any kind of "natural law," but when one analyses their thought their denial is often simply a rejection of any one formulation of these abiding norms or a protest against the idea that man can find a moral ideal by following the bent of his nature, without God's grace.

Most Christians, Protestant and Catholic, believe that there are constants of human behaviour, certain common aspirations of what is deepest in man (and therefore in contact with God) beyond any of the formulated systems of natural law, an inclination produced in the human heart by the God who rules the destiny of men toward their salvation. These constants of human behaviour can serve as the basis of understanding and co-operation for all men. These basic values are precisely *the dignity of the human person* and *the possibility of progress in society*, to which these persons are linked. Both the person and the common good are supreme values. In various periods of history, depending on the self-awareness of men and the evolution of society, the interrelation between the person and the common good was expressed in different sets of laws and institutions, and in this sense we may well speak of an evolution of morality. But behind this development stands the common conviction that man is free and that this freedom implies responsibility to serve the community in which alone the freedom of all is assured.

As a Christian I am very conscious that moral insight or the acknowledgement of these values is due to divine initiative. It is due to God in a direct way through His message addressed to the Church, but it is also due to him, less visibly, through his influence on the hearts of men seeking the right order of the universe. The so-called natural law, therefore, is not based on some definition of human nature, nor on the power of man's reason, nor on the inner harmony of the cosmos, but through man's nature and intelligence, conditioned by his goodwill, on the movement of God in history reconciling humanity with himself.

This leads me to the last question I wish to raise in this brief paper. Do Christians believe in historical progress? Do we believe that the promises which God has made to Israel and which have been fulfilled in Jesus Christ are meant to transform this historical existence of ours, lead men into the concord of one human family, and unify and humanize our life on earth? Here the answer is not easy. All Christians teach that God's action in history draws men to salvation and holiness, preparing them for *the age to come*, and all accept the existence of another force in history, the mystery of evil, the power of human negation which has been with us from the beginning and will remain with us till the end of time. Is it therefore possible to say that the direction of human history is toward greater self-realization? The answer cannot be given from a study of human civilizations, for all apparent progress in this world remains ambiguous. Even the unification of mankind, the humanization and interconnectedness of human life which we witness in our age could be the preparation of a universal revolt against God, a denial of the divine and hence, ultimately, of the truly human. If there is an answer to the question of progress in history, it must, again, be given from a point outside of history.

There are an increasing number of Christian writers in our day, in the Catholic Church and in other Churches, who take so seriously the incarnation of God in Christ, that is, the personal and irrevocable union of God with the human nature of Jesus, that they feel that God has linked himself once and for all to human history. These theologians would appeal to God's universal will to save, revealed in Christ, to the perfect self-surrender of Christ on the cross and the universality of his victory over death and evil, in order to assert that, with the coming of Christ, something irreversible has happened in human history. The whole history of mankind has been re-oriented toward reconciliation with God. These theologians would say, therefore, that it is the mission of the Church to serve humanity in its needs on this earth, to inspire men to find and foster the values common among themselves, and to collaborate in the building of the earthly city, so that the will of God, which is peace and unity, will become more manifest in this world. These writers, then, rejecting the secularistic understanding of progress which has characterized the nineteenth century, and overcoming the inclination to despair so common in modern philosophy, confidently assert that God has established an historical movement in Jesus Christ which is destined to unify and pacify men on this earth.

Reading Pope John's encyclical letter *Pacem in Terris*, addressed to all men of goodwill, one has the impression that this was the vision of the Pope. He believed that it is the mission of the Church to serve the unity of mankind.

GOD AND THE VALUE SCALE*

WILLIAM NICHOLLS

The seventeenth verse of the nineteenth chapter of St. Matthew's Gospel reads: "Why do you ask me about what is good? One is good...." The correct text of the Greek makes the rich young ruler ask a philosophical question or, rather, it makes Jesus reprove him for asking one. "Why do you ask me *about the good*? One is good...." The young man has asked, as you remember, what good thing he should do in order that he might inherit eternal life. Eternal life is not merely that immortal life which a person might hope for beyond death, and it is hardly that at all to a Jew. To him it is a quality of life to be lived first and foremost here and now in this world. The young man is asking, then, in a sense, what is the meaning of life; what is life all about; what is the supreme value, in other words, on which I must stake my life? And Jesus first gives him a very conventional type of reply: "Well, keep the Commandments, follow the moral laws you have been taught." This does not satisfy the young man, for he has been keeping the Commandments ever since the godly upbringing he received from his parents. He is, so far as he is able to judge, a good and a moral person. "Then," says Jesus, "in that case, if you want to be perfect, sell all you have and come with me."

Jesus can speak in this way because as the Messiah, as the Son of God, He is aware of embodying in himself the whole demand and promise of the supreme value itself, Almighty God. One is good and Jesus speaks in his name, and to follow that "One who is good" you may have to forsake every value that you held dear in the past, however good it may be. Jesus does not deny that the moral life which the young man had lived in obedience to the ten commandments, to the traditions of his people, is a good life. Nor, if I read Him aright, does He deny that the rich young ruler's wealth is in itself good and desirable. Affluence, as

*Sunday inter-denominational church address.

such, is a value. It is something which a man may indeed pursue, provided he does not pursue it to the exclusion of all other values. But whether it be the amassing of wealth, gracious living, or whether it be the life of a moral man—these may have to be thrown aside as altogether worthless when a man is confronted with the supreme value itself, with God.

I find myself in a considerable dilemma, for my kind of theologian is not used to talking about values. He sometimes finds that his academic colleagues expect him to be an expert on values. Since this appears to imply that they are the experts on truth and he is left with the values that remain, it is not a very welcome role and, personally, I have always tried to avoid it. I have always tried to say to my colleagues that I know nothing about values. I have no special competence in this field and I should prefer to let a philosopher talk about that. Let me talk about the history which I study or the revelation in which I believe, for both of these are matters of truth. When I try to search my sources as a theologian in the Bible and in what I know of traditional theology, and ask myself where there I find any speech about values, I find myself almost equally baffled. I can find no biblical word to correspond with the notion of value and I am not sure traditional theology really puts the same ideas in words anything like that, even where the ideas indeed do occur. Still, if we are asked the question, I am sure it is our duty to reply. Thus we must see what the word of God has to say, and I think my text, of which I was fortunate enough to be reminded by a friend, may contain the essence of the answer. God alone is the supreme value, and nothing else can be reckoned in the same scale with Him. Other values exist, as I have indicated. Jesus will admit the provisional goodness of morals and of wealth but once make them absolute, once make them into the one controlling principle of life, and they may disrupt the true order of values. This is just as true of morals as it is of wealth.

Nevertheless (and here a conversation about values may become possible to a theologian) this supreme value of God is not evident to all men, not evident certainly to the one who does not believe in God, but also not evident in experience continuously to the Christian. There are times, like the crisis in the life of the rich young ruler, when we may be confronted with the supreme demand of God. We may indeed have to throw away as worthless everything that we have held dear in the sphere of values. But that does not happen to a man very often. There are perhaps sinners and saints who live continuously, as it were, in the presence of the ultimate. Most of us can not bear that and for most of us God prevents that happening. The ultimate, then, is a rare occurrence and though we must always reckon with it, we do not always have to live with it. Surely it is in the realm of the penultimate, of the next-to-the-last things, that values as we usually understand them operate.

Now, as one who tries to expound God's word in the Holy Scriptures, what I have above all to say about values is surely that we must reckon with the possibility of the ultimate entering the lists. When this happens —when God Himself comes upon the scene—then there are no competitors and nothing else can stand beside Him. The first concern of the theologian, then, is to safeguard the rights of this ultimate and to warn against the construction of any value system so watertight that it could exclude the entry of God upon the scene. Thus the reluctance of the theologian to talk about values is not merely an academic game that he plays with his liberally educated friends. It is because he sees in values a genuine danger—the danger of idolatry lest they should be put in the place of God and thus become an obstacle to the truth, and the danger of abstraction. Values are not easy to talk about. As we have all heard on academic and civil occasions, we talk about them as the most boring of abstractions, when we know what seething conflicts are underneath the surface of the values of the institution which is being so pompously commended by the visiting speaker. The danger, then, of abstraction is that values may be separated from the acts and states of men, living men, men as individuals, men in their community relationships, who alone are called to respond to God the supreme value. Abstractions are not of God's creation; they are what our minds do with the truth. But granted this very proper caution of the theologian, this caution which we dare to say we exercise on behalf of God, I do not believe we are wrong in trying to discuss the penultimate, in trying to discuss the realm of the next-to-the-last, which is the best we human beings can do to get to the bottom of things without God. God may come in but until He does, we must cope.

The penultimate then, the realm of the next-to-the-last, is simply the world we all live in, the world in which our ordinary decisions have to be taken, the realm in which it seems we need values. We need to be able to distinguish between the good and the better, between the more and the less, and when I say "we" at this point, I certainly include the Christians amongst the "we." The Christian may rightly hope, I believe, for the aid of God's Holy Spirit in finding his way through the problem of values, but it seems to me that the values through which he hopes the Holy Spirit will lead him, and lead him in such way as never to exclude the possible intervention of God Himself, these values are exactly the same as those that everybody else knows and uses. So the Christian ought not to draw the skirts of his cassock aside and remove himself from the polluted atmosphere of a Conference about values. This is our question, too, little as we may like the language.

The discussion, for us who believe, is certainly relativized, certainly pushed down from the level of ultimate concern, by our knowledge that God is hidden and present throughout the discussion. It is relativized, too, because none other is good but God. No other value can stand in His place at the top. The pyramid of values is truncated without God. The danger involved in leaving God out of account is that of giving the pyramid a false top, of arbitrarily pushing up one of the cluster of values that occupies the second stage, to occupy the place reserved for God alone. Christians often do this, as when they speak and act as if the whole meaning of life lay in morality, instead of God. No, morality is not the whole of life and yet Christians surely are very tempted to think it is. They are very tempted to suppose that morality is the content of what they have to say to the world and, by the same token, falsely to claim a monopoly of moral insight.

I do not think that Christians are the only ones, either, who have attempted to give the pyramid of values a false top. There are plenty of other values which one may be tempted to exalt, and plenty of people who fall into the temptation to do so, but I do not think there is anything inevitable about the secular person falling into that temptation. The secular person may very well accept the logic of his own secularity as I see it, and refuse to admit any ultimate. He is tempted to construct a false ultimate but he need not fall into the temptation. But the importance for our discussion of the refusal to substitute any other ultimate for God is that all the values of the second stage, of what I call the penultimate, or of the second layer of the pyramid, have to share the highest eminence with each other. It follows, therefore, that the cluster of values which are for us the highest that we can know, remains a cluster, a plurality of values, which cannot be reduced to each other, are therefore relative to each other, and, finally, are inevitably in conflict. The conflict of values, therefore, is a universal human experience for the simple reason that no one value can claim the place of God. All these different values that we can experience and elucidate are good; they all have their own claim upon our attention and action; and in real life we are always trying to balance good against good and to choose as best we can unless it should happen, as it happened to the rich young ruler, that God should unmistakably intervene and end the debate about values with His own "Follow Me."

What, then, are these secondary, "penultimate" values? I do not think I need to speak about them very long. Morality or goodness is one of them and if you want to complete the familiar triad with truth and beauty, I have no objection. However, I should remind you that you cannot reduce one of these to any of its fellows, and I am not altogether convinced by the suggestion of the poet that they are really forms of the same thing. You cannot for example, reduce beauty to goodness; the attempt to be moral about aesthetics leads to bad aesthetic judgments. Nor, for that matter, can truth be reduced to beauty, for the truth may be ugly and we may have to face very unwelcome and displeasing truths.

Rather, each of these three may, from time to time, occupy the first place in our life and then be dethroned as another assumes the greatest importance. We may think we are devoted to truth but one day we may find that compassion requires the withholding of at least part of the truth. A man, for example, is not truly moral if he does not understand that he may have to lie to save his friend. And even goodness, in this world, must at times have to take second place, possibly to truth. There may be a time when the truth must be told, when the truth must be pursued, even if we do not know how to do that by the ways we have thought of as good. Christians nowadays often try to take love as the supreme value. Yet I am not quite convinced that even this will work, for, even if we leave aside the claim of beauty, surely love cannot lord it over truth. Love, without truth, as Cardinal Leger said at the Fourth World Conference on Faith and Order, is blind and may lead us to false and sentimental distortions of love. Moreover, while Christians certainly must say that God is love, we are not for that reason authorized to say that love is God.

Values, then, will in this world always be in conflict until God resolves our dilemma. God will resolve it, if He does, in His own way and that way will be valid for every individual when it happens to him. And it may come, as I have suggested, by the overthrowing of even our most cherished goods and by the revelation that to the very extent we have cherished them they have become idols that kept us from God, or it may come in the demand for the consecration of values which we have previously understood in isolation from God, their Giver.

Nevertheless since to live we must in fact do something about resolving the conflict, we ought to ask what the Christian is able to say about the ordering of the values of this world. Clearly, the Christian will understand all values as ordered to God who is their apex, their source. But human life is human, and the values out of which the pyramid is built are the same values for all men. The Christian knows, however, that God is man's Creator and Redeemer. Man may be the measure of the values which we affirm but man did not create himself and man cannot get himself out of his own alienation from God, from his neighbour, and from himself and his work. *God* made man; *God* reconciles man to Himself; knowing this will at certain points bring the values of the Christian into the sharpest possible alignment. "Man does not live by bread alone but by every word that proceedeth out of the mouth of God." The values of a material culture are good but without God they are not enough. Or from the same passage, that of the temptations of Jesus, "Thou shalt worship the Lord thy God, Him only shalt thou serve." The state is good but the state can never demand of the Christian an absolute loyalty. True as it is that the values of the Christian may at times be brought into this sharp alignment, at most times the Christian will share the conflict in which others find themselves. And I do not come before you this morning as an oracle who can resolve all these conflicts for you. I cannot resolve my own, but I must try to do so if I recognize the validity of the conflict.

Finally, something about the personal life. There is in the Christian mind at the moment a great revolt against this style of life which we have inherited from the past. We feel that the traditional Christian piety is stuffy and unreal. We often become critical of it, but we have not yet substituted for it a contemporary style of Christian life. We may be on the way to finding one. Too much Christian piety either has been withdrawn from the real world in which ordinary people have to live, or has blessed the values in the society in which we live by accepting conventional morality, or success, and often financial success at that, as a sign of a person's integrity before God. What is surely clear, especially today, is that we need a most searching honesty going right down into the depths of the emotional life and the soul; and this searching honesty, which is as hard to come by for a Christian as anybody else, is the only thing that is going to keep this style of life free from the taint of hypocrisy.

Work is a difficult thing to talk about because here too we are almost always prone to self-righteousness. Perhaps the greatest blessing I feel I have in my own life, apart from the gift of my own nearest and dearest, is that I like my work, that I can live to work instead of working to live. But there are a great many people in the world for whom work is a ceaseless monotony giving no hope whatever except of an increased pay cheque, and in the present order of our society I do not know how that can be avoided; but while it cannot be avoided, let us not talk too big about the holiness of work.

Then, in the sphere of personal and social ethics, I think social ethics have been very much undervalued by Christians. Here, too, we have the pietistic perversion which gives us an exaggerated personal scrupulousness coupled with a great social irresponsibility. In other words, we worry terribly about whether we have broken some taboo in our personal life and do not care at all about the sufferings of millions of our fellow creatures. The Marxists, I believe, are apt to be a bit scornful about a personal morality that is not ordered toward the social good. I think we can learn a little from them at that point without necessarily throwing over what is good in our personal lives. In the Christian understanding of social morality, we have to take as a norm the fact that man is meant for community, a community with God and neighbour. And so the Christian morality of society is based on the idea of the person in community, which is opposed to either individualism on the one hand or collectivism on the other. I am sure this cuts political ice. In the discussions of our own time we ought not to play off individual liberty against social justice, nor to play off the value of private charity against the acceptance of social responsibility in a welfare society. I am perfectly sure that there is, in fact, no restriction of genuine personal freedom involved in the acceptance of social responsibility. I think we might take it as the Christian axiom for society that the adult, the fit, and the productive ought to support the young, the old, the sick, and the unemployed, and that this is not a matter of charity, not something to be raised by Red Feather schemes and so on, but a matter of elementary justice which has to be organized by society as a whole. Until we fulfil those ideas of justice we are not in a position to talk about charity.

The Christian, then, is called to follow God, is called to see in God a value so immense as to dwarf all others. Yet he is called to follow God for the most part in the ordinary life of this world with his fellow beings, and he is no better than they, no more blessed with insight, no more blessed with moral resources than his fellows except in so far as he is able to depend upon God. We are all, it seems to me, at one at this moment in our puzzlement over the conflict of values. The Christian Church, sensitive as it always has been to the cultural changes going on all around it, is going through a time of re-thinking its own traditional values out of which something very important and new may be emerging (I think there are signs of it already). But in the meantime, for this Conference, we theologians who bear the Christian name, who believe in the Christian God, want to waive any supposed privilege and allow ourselves to be, as we are, equals with our fellow men: *unless God should speak.*

THE POLITICAL MEANING OF LIBERTY AND EQUALITY

GIOVANNI SARTORI

What is the relevance of what I can say to an audience which lives thousands of miles away from my country? I am a European who lives in Italy, and this means in the very fringe of the democratic hemisphere. Where I live one has the feeling—which is both unpleasant and exciting —of being dangerously exposed; whereas surely you do not have the same feeling in Canada. Canada is, as I see it in comparison to Italy, a lovely, happy, protected corner of the West. Personally, I feel strongly about values, and about political values in particular—but do Canadians?

This, to be sure, is a question which I shall have to leave unanswered. I did find, however, a reason for coming to Canada. It is rather doubtful, I am afraid, whether our present-day world will allow safe and quiet corners to survive. Only short distances remain, for long, long distances have become short. It has taken me just about seven hours to cross the Atlantic from London to Toronto. In warfare terms, that is, with military vehicles, the whole of the Western hemisphere can be covered in a couple of hours, more or less. Long distances have become short and this fact implies that we must begin to think of each other as Westerners, as belonging to the same civilization, as Walter Lippmann says, and as having a common destiny. If Europe is in trouble, then North America is in trouble too. In this sense, we have common problems, and this is why I perhaps have something to contribute to this Conference.

The general title of the Conference is "Values in Conflict," but the specific title on which I have been asked to comment is just "Values in the Political Sphere." The word conflict has been omitted. (As you can see right away, I'm very pedantic-minded!) I understand, therefore, that I am left with the responsibility of deciding whether political values belong, or do not belong, to the general class "values in conflict." My reply is simple enough: of course they do. Nevertheless, it is expedient to make a distinction between an *external* and an *internal* conflict. By external conflict, I mean the conflict between the West and the East. By internal conflict, I mean the conflict among ourselves, among Westerners. In the first sense, we are confronted with two very different ideals of the good life, of the political good life; namely, the conflict "democracy versus Communism." In the second sense, we have to take stock of the fact that within the Western world itself we are bitterly divided, and that some of us, or even many of us, have become uncertain about the validity of the values our fathers professed.

I shall confine myself to the latter issue, and there is a good reason for this, for there is little chance of winning the external conflict, or the over-all conflict, unless we are able to settle, beforehand, our internal problems and difficulties. As things now stand, the conflict of values between East and West, between Communism and liberal democracy, is mostly a one-way fight in which one army is adhesive and aggressive, while the other army is divided and soft. Let us face it: the spirit of the West taken as a whole is hardly a fighting spirit. One reason for this is that we have become uncertain about the value of our values. The other reason can be summed up in this question: are we still really interested and concerned with values?

Values are not a thing, they are not a material entity. Values are ideals which exist only in so far as people believe in them, and are prepared to fight for them. If not, we simply have no values. We have a situation of "value vacuum," so to speak. Is this the case? I shall not try to answer this question. I would start saying nasty things, and I have been taught, when I was being educated, that this is a bad start. Let us just pose the problem and try to pinpoint some specific issues.

According to my pedantic mind, the first query is bound to be: which values are political values? I shall follow Tocqueville in replying that the basic political values of our times are the value of *liberty* and the value of *equality*. Another way of putting the problem is to ask (I am now quoting Bertrand Russell): "How can we combine the degree of individual initiative which is necessary for progress, with the degree of social cohesion which is necessary for survival?" In this approach, the terms are, then, the *individual* and *society*. This latter approach is in many ways related to the former one, for when we speak of liberty we usually mean liberty for the individual, whereas when we speak of equality we usually refer to the claims of society *upon* individuals. From this angle too, Tocqueville, ever prophetic, posed the problem in a masterly fashion. He wrote: "Our forefathers were ever prone to make an improper use of the notion that private rights ought to be respected. And we are naturally prone on the other hand to exaggerate the idea that the interests of the private individual ought always to bend to the interests of the many." Would one suspect that this sentence was written over a century ago?

Despite the close connection between the values of liberty and equality, on the one hand, and the concepts of individual and society, on the other hand, I shall stick to the first framework: liberty and equality. The trouble with the other conceptualization is that, while the term individual is clear enough, the term society is very confusing indeed. We are therefore likely to get stuck in problems such as these: what comes first, the tree, or the forest? One will say: can there be a forest without trees? And another will answer: of course not, but the single tree is an irrelevant entity as compared to the whole, to the forest. As anyone can see, we are not likely to go very far in this kind of discussion. And this is why I much prefer to consider our basic values in terms of liberty and equality.

By this I do not mean in the least that the concepts of liberty and equality are simple and clear concepts. I only mean that they can be discussed and analysed more fruitfully. A second caution is necessary. Only at a very high level of abstraction can one conceive liberty and equality as being eternal and unchanging values, given once and for all. The more we come down to earth, the more we have to speak of specific liberties (in the plural), and of specific equalities (also in the plural); and the more we come to realize that these specific liberties and equalities also have a dynamic dimension. Not a too dynamic dimension, however. Values and value-beliefs cannot change too much and too rapidly. If they do, or when they do, this simply means that certain ideals and aspirations have not really gained the status of values, or else that they are losing the status of values. I must emphasize, in this connection, that values are a terribly serious matter. They decide the growth and fall of civilizations. They are a way of representing what a civilization is, and what it shall and can do. So, in this sense, there is an element—in basic value-beliefs—that remains unchanged under the most changing conditions. I shall concentrate on this unchanging essence of the values of liberty and equality.

The second query in my list is: what do liberty and equality mean, that is, how do I define these concepts? Despite endless disputes on this matter, I still maintain that the concept of political liberty, or political freedom, is not an ambiguous concept, provided there are some preliminary clarifications.

In the first place, let it be clear that we are concerned with political freedom; not with the over-all problem of freedom, and in particular not with the philosophical and metaphysical queries concerning the "true nature" or the "ultimate essence" of freedom. These are indeed vital queries, but we are not concerned, in the political sphere, with the problem of the freedom of the will, or the like. Whether our will is free or not, whether we are free agents or not, the problem of political freedom remains the problem of making sure that no man (I am now quoting Locke) is "subject to the inconstant, uncertain, unknown, arbitrary will of another man." So my first warning is: political liberty is not a philosophical kind of liberty, and is definitely not the practical solution of a philosophical problem.

In the second place, and this is my second warning, let us make sure that we are placed in the correct optic. The problem of political freedom arises only when we approach the relation between citizen and state *from the point of view of the citizens*. If we consider this relation from the point of view of the power-holders, we are no longer concerned with political freedom. The sentence "The state is free" (implying that it can do anything it wishes to) amounts to saying that the citizen is not free. Let me put it thus: citizens are free to the extent that the state is unfree, that is, to the extent that the power addressees are able to control and to curb the power of the power holders.

In the third place, let me suggest a very simple rule of thumb for detecting the core of political freedom. When we find ourselves in the fortunate situation of being free, after some time the generations who have inherited liberty *gratis* become very sophisticated about it. We start saying that political freedom is not only a negative freedom, that is, a freedom *from*, but also a positive freedom, that is, a freedom *to*. However, no sooner is freedom lost, than people go back to the very plain definition of freedom which was given by Hobbes. Freedom, wrote Hobbes, "is the absence of external impediments." Why, of all authors, have I chosen to quote Hobbes? Surely, he was not campaigning for liberalism. But he happened to live in a time in which there was very little freedom. And therefore Hobbes well understood what political liberty was about. So the simple rule I am suggesting is the following: that whenever we have to reply to the question "what is political freedom?" we should approach the problem *as if* we were being oppressed, that is, assuming that we have lost our freedom. If one surveys the literature on liberty, one does find a large variety of definitions whenever the authors consulted enjoyed a situation of freedom; but one finds also an astonishing continuity of meaning whenever the writers were subject to tyrannical rule. Whenever people have not been free, they have defined political freedom as a freedom *from*, as absence of external impediments, or, in other terms still, as freedom from coercion, as non-restraint. To be sure, these definitions should not be taken too literally. The absence of restriction is not absence of *all* restriction. The absence of coercion is not the absence of *every* coercion. The answers to the questions "protected from what?" and "unrestricted to what extent?" depend on what is at stake at a given time and place, and also on what is most valued, or more intensely valued, in a particular society. This does not detract from the fact that any definition of freedom which neglects to mention that political freedom is basically a protective freedom, a freedom *from* much more than a freedom *to*, is likely to be a definition of some other freedom, not of political freedom.

Let us come to the definition of equality. Equality is indeed an ambiguous notion, a Janus-faced concept. In one sense it is a moral ideal, but in another sense it is not; it simply conveys the idea of likeness. The definition of equality can be developed in the sense that we seek justice, but also in the sense that we seek identity. On the one hand the ideal of equality stems from the principle "to each his due," but on the other hand it leads us to dislike variety, diversity, and dissent. Clearly, the two meanings are mutually conflicting; but it is not easy to unravel them and to separate them neatly. The overlapping of "equality-as-justice" with "equality-of-sameness" is less evident in English than it is in French, Italian, or German. I mean that while the French *égal*, the Italian *eguale*, and the German *gleich* mean both "equal" and "same," English-speaking people do not usually say that two billiard balls are "equal," meaning that they are "alike." Nevertheless, the English vocabulary of politics also mingles the idea of equality with the idea of sameness, probably out of the translations of continental authors. For instance, to cite a well-known text, Lincoln's Springfield speech of 1857 affirms that the authors of the Declaration of Independence "did not intend to declare all men equal in all respects. They did not mean to say that all were equal in colour, size, intellect, moral development or social capacity." Now, let us reflect a minute: Lincoln is simply saying that the founding fathers did not mean to say that all men are alike. And, clearly, his explanation would have been altogether superfluous if the equation between the moral and the physical meaning of equality had not occurred in English parlance as well. How obvious, if one comes to think of it! Yes, it is obvious—but nevertheless this equation is still at the very core of our present-day perplexities and misunderstandings.

Having cleared the way, we may now come to what troubles our minds and divides us—to our internal value conflict. The question is:

how can we successfully balance liberty with equality? How can the free individual co-exist with, and within, an egalitarian society? He can, upon two conditions, I venture to suggest.

In the first place equality combines with freedom only when it is not understood as uniformity. For if we seek sameness, we are bound to dislike diversity, and if we dislike diversity we cannot praise freedom (except by being flagrantly inconsistent—as is often the case). The liberal democratic formula is not "unequal opportunities to become equal," but, vice versa, "equal opportunities to become unequal." The liberal democratic principle is that we must oppose fictitious and undeserved equalities just as much, and exactly for the same reason, that we must oppose unjustified and unjust inequalities. Our value of equality calls for unchecked mobility, for equal opportunities; it does not call for a uniform leveling, for making men as identical as billiard balls are.

The second condition is that the relationship between liberty and equality be understood properly. Most people are excited about the question: what is more important, liberty or equality? My own opinion is that this is not the question. For it is rather obvious that if people are free and unequal, they will give more importance to equality (that is, to what they do not have); whereas if people are equal but unfree, they will give more importance to liberty (as was the case with slaves, who are, let us remember it, a good example of the kind of equality that somebody seems eager to provide for us). So the real question does not concern an order of *preference* but an order of *precedence*—which is a very different thing. And, in procedural terms, there is no doubt, I believe, that liberty comes first.

To conclude: the above does not imply in the least that liberty is to be preferred. It implies only that the relationship between liberty and equality is, procedurally speaking, a one-way relationship. Through liberty we can obtain equality. But the contrary is not true. Starting from equality, liberty will not necessarily follow. Political freedom defined as absence of external impediments, as freedom *from*, is only a beginning—I grant that. But a beginning that cannot be by-passed. If I am not permitted to do what I wish, nothing follows, and this is the end of the story.

DEMOCRACY AND NATIONALISM: THE CANADIAN CONFLICT

FRANK UNDERHILL

I propose to limit my remarks to our own country of Canada, taking Canada as a sort of case study for the purpose of throwing some incidental light upon two of our main Western political values: democracy and nationalism. That is, I am fighting as a local militiaman in a small local engagement which is only part of a great world battle.

Canada is a liberal democracy. We are devoted alike to liberty and to equality; and the insoluble problem of the relationship between these two polar ideals of democratic society does not seem to have caused us much unhappiness. We have gone through no great revolutions in our past in order to achieve these liberal-democratic values, nor have we made any great sacrifices which would permanently endear these values to us. We have not contributed in any noteworthy way to influence the minds of men by great books or other writing on the meaning of liberalism and democracy, liberty and equality. There is no Canadian thinker, philosopher, prophet, or seer who is known outside his own country for his reflections on these high subjects—or, for that matter, inside his own country.

This must surely mean that we have not felt or experienced in any profound way the values which are embodied in our political institutions and habits, and to which we profess devotion. Of course, if we wish to indulge in self-flattery, we may claim that our values are so stable, so deep-rooted, that there is no need to write about them, fight about them, or even think about them.

Confederation was brought about in 1867 by the leadership of a small elite of political groups in the various British American colonies. This elite was in advance of the masses of its fellow citizens. There was little of that American element, "we, the People," in the making of the Canadian constitution. The Quebec Resolutions were not submitted for approval to general elections, referenda, or plebiscites of the voters in the confederating provinces. The Fathers of Confederation did not profess to be democrats. All of them were opposed to such American democratic practices as manhood suffrage and the election of executive and judicial officials.

The rebellions in the two Canadas in 1837 had indeed been inspired by these American democratic ideas—for this was the period in the United States of Jacksonian democracy, of the rise of the common man to a share in political power. Mackenzie wanted to set up a government in Upper Canada which would spring directly from and would be directly responsible to the little men, to the mechanics in the towns and the farmers beyond the ridges, and which would not be controlled by the narrow governing cliques in Toronto and other urban centres whom he called the Upper Canada Family Compact. But he was easily defeated, as was Papineau in Lower Canada. In the 1840's we went in for "Responsible Government" rather than for Jacksonian democracy, that is, for a British Whig parliamentary form of government under the leadership of the best people. To Mackenzie, and to the Grits who followed him in the 1850's and 1860's, this elite consisted of the upper bourgeoisie of commerce, finance, transportation, and industry in place of the old elite of the land-speculating pseudo-aristocracy of the Family Compact.

Yet today, one hundred years later, we have become largely a populist democracy on the American model. No one can remember when manhood suffrage was adopted. Our society is equalitarian, like American society. We have no relics of a feudal aristocracy or an established church (at least in English Canada). We have refused to worry very much about the rise of an oligarchic plutocracy. We congratulate ourselves that democracy has housebroken our plutocracy. We have failed to develop any strong class feeling; political parties based on class appeals have not got very far. Because of this we have been the despair of good Marxians.

What we have been doing, however, is gradually transforming our parliamentary system into a plebiscitary democracy. Our elections become plebiscites on the choice of a national leader, like American presidential elections. The leader's appeal depends essentially not on his policies or his party but on the question whether the ordinary man and his wife can identify themselves with him. A leader who has proved himself completely bankrupt in policies and administrative capacity can still collect 33 per cent of the popular votes on the slogan that everybody is against him but the people. The emergence of the Social Credit movement and of the Diefenbaker Conservative movement, with their appeal to the little men in the small towns and on the farms, to the more uneducated and backward sections of the population, with their suspicion of Civil Service experts and central bankers, with their fundamentalist anti-intellectualism in both religion and politics—all this shows how far we have gone in the direction of a simple-minded populist democracy.

This means that the philosopher to whom we should have paid most attention in Canada for the light he throws upon our politics is not Marx but Tocqueville. It was in the early 1830's that Tocqueville came out from France to the United States to study how equalitarian democracy works. As an aristocrat who recognized defeat, he had decided that this was the form of society toward which all Western countries were moving. He found that equality was still compatible with freedom in America as it had not been in revolutionary France.

But he was alarmed by the lack of intellectual and moral distinction in American society, by the tendency to conformity, by the worship of public opinion, by the belief that it was one's duty to accept the standards —intellectual, moral, and spiritual—of the ordinary commonplace man. He thought that this would make for the undermining in the long run of individual autonomy and liberty. The danger facing American society was not from the tyranny of a despot or an oligarchy, but from the steady, gentle, unrelenting pressure of a majoritarian democracy. Tocqueville did not invent the term, but he had already discovered in the 1830's that North Americans are "other-directed." As we read him today we cannot help being impressed by his uncannny insight into the underlying tendencies of this continent toward populist democracy. He studied the eastern United States closely and got as far west through the back woods as Green Bay. You could almost say that he foresaw everything that has since happened in America except the Green Bay Packers. They represent a form of austre disciplined excellence which he did not anticipate.

Of course, it is only too easy for modern culture-snobs to get into the habit of condemning the masses. If we do not maintain our faith in the powers of judgment of the common man when he is fairly presented with a choice between alternatives and in his ability to rise to a crisis, we have ceased to be democrats. Nevertheless the growing technological complexity of our modern society must drive us to some modification of our populist democracy. Modern society simply will not work without technical experts in charge of all its complicated machinery, without trained administrators, without a highly sophisticated elite of men and women who have undergone a rigorous intellectual discipline. Modern industrial production makes for hierarchy and bureaucracy in social organization, and there is no escape from this. Nothing, in fact, is so likely to drive an intelligent observer to despair of simple democracy as to watch that representative cross-section of our Canadian populist democracy, the 265 members of the House of Commons, trying to deal with our current problems.

We are approaching a new form of society to which the old terms of aristocracy, democracy, plutocracy, are no longer relevant. We are developing into a meritocratic society, at the head of which is a directing elite composed of persons selected for their merit after prolonged intellectual training in our schools and universities. This elite has not yet solidified into a self-conscious distinct social group. How it is to fit in with our established populist democracy is a problem that we have not yet solved. The most fatal thing that could happen would be for a cleavage to develop between the meritocracy and the masses of the people. I do not know the answer to this problem. I only know that anti-intellectualism is the dominant North American form of original sin.

There is another aspect to this question of democratic values inside Canada to which we have never given sufficient attention. Democracy means, it must mean when every citizen is given a voice in decision-making, majority rule. But in a free society it must also mean minority rights. How do you reconcile these two values in a community like ours which is divided into a permanent majority, the English Canadians, and a permanent minority, the French Canadians? A little more than one hundred years ago the United States was divided on similar lines over the question of slavery; it found itself unable to settle this issue by democratic processes, and resorted to coercion and civil war. Before the war came, Calhoun of South Carolina tried to solve the problem by his doctrine of "concurrent majorities." On certain vital issues, he maintained, the majority must not adopt policies without the consent of the minority. But on the vital issue of slavery this meant giving a veto to the Southern minority. The North found the doctrine of concurrent majorities intolerable, and imposed its majority will upon the Southern minority.

Here in Canada, our French Canadians, without ever having heard of Calhoun, have for a century been adherents of the doctrine of concurrent majorities. But in 1917 on the issue of conscription the French minority and the English majority almost broke apart completely. Are there any issues on which the French minority has a veto?—and if so what are they? The essence of Canadian statesmanship has always been to keep the two communal groups going along together in some kind of an amicable relationship so as to avoid this issue of majority rule versus minority rights. On the whole the French have protected their minority rights by taking care to be part of the majority political party that, at any given time, rules the country. But now this system of a bi-cultural political party as a means of communal harmony seems to be breaking down, because the French claim that we English Canadians have abused our majority position to condemn them to a permanent status of second-class citizens, and there is talk of secession. Isn't there something ironical in the fact that in this year, 1963, one hundred years after the battle of Gettysburg which settled the claim of a minority to secede from the United States, we should have a minority here in Canada talking ever more insistently about secession?

Discussion of French-English relations inside Canada leads naturally to the topic of Canadian nationalism. The Dominion of Canada was born rather late in the day during the great century of nationalism, the nineteenth century. Its first government, composed of French as well as of English cabinet ministers, in the speech from the throne in the first session of the first parliament, proclaimed that "a new nationality" had come into being. Nationality was taken by everyone in those days to be the final form in which a people consolidated themselves in order to live the good life. Man was born to realize his highest potentialities as a citizen of the democratic national state.

Today, one hundred years after our new nationality was so hopefully established, we are engaged in a bitter and searching discussion of the meaning of nationalism. The spokesmen of French Canada seem to be claiming that there is no such thing as a pan-Canadian nation, but only a bi-national federal state, consisting of two nations, one French-speaking and one English-speaking. It was not a new Canadian nationality that was formed in 1867, according to this French doctrine, but only an Austro-Hungarian Dual Monarchy. Or rather that is what is to be formed in the proposed reconstruction of Confederation that is to take place before July 1, 1967—or else.

Of course it is foolish to put too much emphasis on the meaning of the word "nation," but it seems to me that these French spokesmen are reverting to an earlier, more primitive, and simplicist conception of nationality than that which our leaders, French as well as English, had reached in 1867. Nationality to these modern French Canadians is based on race, language, and religion. Our forefathers were experimenting with something more complex, more difficult, and also more interesting and creative, a nation that would consist of two main communal groups but would not be based on the traditional ties of race, language, or religion, but on the more subtle ties of the experience of living together, pursuing common purposes as one people, each group finding its life enriched by intercourse with the other group. Perhaps their reach exceeded our grasp. This is a mournful conclusion after an experiment which has lasted for a hundred years.

A nation, said Renan—and Renan, I suppose, is hardly a persuasive authority to quote to French Catholics—is a group of people who have done great things together in the past and who hope to do great things together in the future. The life of a nation, he went on, is a daily plebiscite. Its continuance depends upon this common consent, constantly renewed. In 1867 we had done great things together in the past. We had won responsible government. We had pre-empted the northern half of the North American continent from further American expansion. In 1967, will there be no great things for us to do together in the future? The ultimate question that faces us is to which of these two conceptions of nationality we shall give our allegiance: the narrower, self-centred, parochial one, or the wider, more complex, and more difficult one?

The more moderate Quebec nationalists insist that we must not confuse them with the extremists, the separatists. But the distinction becomes at times rather difficult for an outsider to understand. They are not thinking of secession, say the moderates, and then show that that is just what some of them are thinking of when they warn us in portentous tones that they may be driven to it if we do not grant their demands for "Reconfederation."

Just what is involved in reconfederation does not seem to have been very clearly defined as yet. But let us be clear about one thing. In a free community such as Canada, reconfederation can be brought about only by negotiation among the parties concerned; and negotiation involves compromise and concession by both sides. To judge from some of the speeches that are reported from the other side of the Ottawa River, there seems to be a naive romantic idea in some quarters that reconfederation means that the spokesmen of Quebec will present the rest us with their new terms, we shall agree, and we shall all live happily ever afterwards. That is not what real politics is like. In genuine negotiation both sides have to accept terms that they do not like.

Nor is genuine negotiation carried on by a process in which one side presents ultimata, lays down time limits within which agreement must be reached, and ends each statement of its claims with an ominous "or else." This is the way in which the Russian Communists have usually negotiated with us; and of course, it is obvious that they adopt these tactics because they don't want to reach an agreement.

Any form of union between the French-speaking group and the English-speaking group must ultimately be based on an underlying conviction in each group that the interests and sentiments which unite us are more important than those which divide us. This is what English Canadians mean when they talk about a Canadian nation. Surely our union over the last hundred years must have been based upon a conviction of this kind in the minds and hearts of the substantial majority of both groups. And here we come to the crux of the issue today. We are involved in something deeper than a semantic discussion about the meaning of the word "nation." If this conviction about the underlying importance of the things that unite us no longer exists in the minds and hearts of the people of Quebec, then we are heading for a tragic disaster in Canada—and it will be tragic for French Canadians as well as for English Canadians.

It seems to me, also, that many of the Quebec nationalists, when they become so passionate about maintaining the individual identity of their culture, are indulging in romantic fantasies about the possibility of a separatist, inward-looking culture among any people that wants to be modern in our twentieth-century world. There are too many cultural influences today which cross and re-cross national boundaries for a doctrinaire cultural separatism to be viable. And this, of course, is something which we English Canadians need to remember also when we reject opportunities to learn the French language and to enrich our own culture by contacts with French-Canadian culture. Cultural interrelationships may be dangerous, but cultural isolationism is in the long run fatal.

It is for reasons such as these that the conflicting values involved in the question of nationalism confront us Canadians with the responsibility of making the most critical decisions that we shall be called upon to make in the next few years.

All of which leads me to my last point. While we are agonizing over this domestic issue of nationality, it is becoming obvious that these particularist independent nationalities, big or little, form one of the chief obstacles in the way of a peaceful, stable, world community. As Arnold Toynbee keeps repeating to us, our contemporary world of nation-states is in the same condition today as was the Hellenic world of independent city states in the fourth century B.C. They could not achieve a wider loyalty than that to their particularist city-states, and they disappeared as significant entities. Today science and technology, industry, commerce and transportation, scholarship and learning, population movements of all kinds, are creating bonds among peoples which stretch across national boundaries. Something greater is demanded of us than national loyalties.

Our Fathers of Confederation in 1867 created something new. The best way in which we can commemorate their work in our centenary celebrations of 1967 is to imitate their spirit and to bend our energies to creating something new, some wider form of human association than the national state. Who was it who said that nationalism is the measles of mankind and should be gotten over with early in life? Alas, I fear that we are in for a rather severe attack of measles on our hundredth birthday.

THE VALIDITY OF PREVAILING
ECONOMIC VALUES

THOMAS BALOGH

The fact that the conflict of values in the economic sphere has been included in this series, and that the conflict contemplated was not a conventional defence of the Western values against the Communist, should permit us to be a little optimistic. We shall not follow the well-worn path of the psychological-warfare warriors of the "Council for Cultural Freedom," that well-endowed body of men who nobly fight for liberty and try to discredit anyone opposing them as disloyal. We shall turn to the much more satisfying and important task of discovering how to make our values prevail in our actions. This change in approach shows the progress that has been made in the Western world in the last few years. It permits us to hope that we shall be able to face successfully the Communist challenge both on the moral and on the material plane.

At the same time, the fact that the conflict in values in the economic sphere has been included brings back to mind the great tradition of classical economists who, whatever might have been their views, had the right attitude to their subject. Not for them were the evasions and pseudo-scientism of present-day pure and mathematical economics. They knew that if their subject was to mean anything at all it would have to be political economy in close touch with the historical and social reality of the day, providing not worthless models, non-existing logical constructions whose only criterion was consistence and elegance, but a living positive doctrine to be applied here and now to the organic and living tissue of everyday existence.

In contrast, modern economics, especially in America, and especially since the convulsions of the McCarthy period, has not yet recovered from the retreat into mathematical formulae which served to give it political security: for no one would accuse mathematical tautologies of subversion. It has been voided of relevance until the large part of contemporary contributions represents little more than ingenious variations on inapplicable themes.

The basis of the great classical school further developed by Marshall and his followers was the identification of our basic moral values, "liberty, equality, and fraternity," as well as the "pursuit of happiness," with the unfettered working of the market based on private property and individual risk-bearing. It was, for the elite, a comfortable doctrine. Adam Smith's invisible hand bestowed not merely the maximum possible satisfaction to all, dominated by the sovereign consumer; it also secured human dignity. It would in the end bring about even equality. In the meantime, it would remunerate all factors of production, land, capital, and labour, exactly in proportion to their contribution to the product. Economics, moreover, unlike other less scientific social sciences, could prove this not merely qualitatively but quantitatively. Until recently, economists and for that matter the general public did not question the nature of the relationship between production and the "welfare," or satisfaction, toward which the socio-economic organization and policy are supposed to be directed. Explicitly or implicitly, increased *production* was taken as a certain proof of increasing *welfare*. It seemed common sense. On the basis of a few assumptions, which sounded eminently sensible, a profound and complicated structure was built up. This purported to provide a fully developed theory of consumers' demand and enabled the economist to give determinate answers to policy questions.

How was this done? It was recognized, of course, that in these basic questions of human existence the relation of means to ends is far from precise or simple; a fundamental decision about values was needed. In the Western world, the final dignity and happiness of the individual as such is acclaimed as the basic principle. This is the fundamental Christian belief from which all politico-economic enquiry must start. We are prone to proclaim it with fervour.

But men do not live on their ultimate dignity. They are members of society and, as such, require also the means of keeping themselves alive and providing material goods and services needed for existence. Between man as consumer, as the recipient of aesthetic and material pleasures, and as producer, as the member of a tightly knit and hierarchically organized team, there is a deep chasm. Contradictions might arise and the economist might then not be able to provide objective answers.

The neo-classical writers slide over these difficulties with consummate elegance. The many-sidedness of human existence, they explain patiently, is such that all problems cannot be tackled at once. Drastic simplification, firm disregard of the complications introduced by the investigations of the specialists, seems defensible, indeed essential, in order to reduce to some sort of order the chaotic multitude of facts.

For economists to be able to provide definite answers to problems of choice between different social and political policies, it suffices to assume that *general* welfare is somehow *uniquely* related to something called *economic* welfare, which itself is capable of measurement, and further that economic welfare can be measured by valuing production on the basis of market prices.

The late Professor Pigou, the originator of modern welfare economics, provides a typical example of this method. He begins with a modest statement: "A general investigation of all the groups of causes by which welfare thus conceived [i.e. general welfare] may be affected would constitute a task so enormous and complicated as to be quite impracticable. . . ." He goes on to say:

> The one obvious instrument of measurement in social life is money. Hence the range of our enquiry becomes restricted to that part of social welfare that can be brought directly or indirectly, into relation with the measuring rod of money. This part of welfare may be called economic welfare.

> Though no precise boundary between economic and non-economic welfare exists, yet the test of accessibility to a money measure serves well enough to set up a rough distinction. Economic welfare, as loosely defined by this test is the subject-matter of economic science. The purpose of this volume [*Economics of Welfare*] is to study certain important groups of causes that affect economic welfare in actual modern societies.[1]

He admits and names some grounds why "economic welfare will not serve for a barometer or index of total welfare." But in the end he rejects these objections with the engaging reflection that after all "full guidance for practice requires . . . capacity to carry out quantitative and not merely qualitative analysis." In order, that is, to be able to make use of his own formal conclusions he asserts without any further ado or analysis that the "burden of proof" lies upon those who hold that "the presumption should be overruled" that "measurable and non-measurable welfare in [his] sense are similarly affected by the same cause."

This sounds sensible and scientific and has been accepted as such by the overwhelming majority of all writers. Prices, after all, would reflect the consumers' needs, tastes, and urgency of demand, and competition between producers would ensure that no one could claim more than was his due. It was all very simple and satisfying.

On a closer look this procedure becomes untenable in more than one

[1] Pigou, A., *The Economics of Welfare*, London, Macmillan, 1932, p. 11.

respect. It is not true first of all that the yardstick of money can measure accurately the relative social urgency of demand and satisfaction. Nor is it true that free competition assures a just distribution of the product. Monopoly of power, the growth of the productive unit, the inequality of wealth and opportunity, not least through inequality of education, training, and influence, have vitiated any inherent tendency to equality which the system may have had. Unemployment and insecurity are besetting blemishes of the system, but their elimination seems incompatible with the assurance of stability. Since the war we have alternated between periods of inflation and unemployment—and often we have been beset by both at the same time.

The price system moreover cannot express adequately those indirect gains which accrue to the community as a whole through the action of its members. Yet these have become steadily more important as have collective needs. No doubt these changes have been the result of the success of the individualist system, of our growing affluence. But they can no longer be disregarded.

Indeed they have undermined the very basis of economics. In order that market prices may provide an acceptable measure of social values on the consumer side, it is necessary not merely that consumers should be rational and consistent but that their tastes should be given and unchangeable. Their satisfaction must not be influenced by other people's consumption. It must be decided entirely by their own. The consumer, as the sociological jargon goes, must be entirely inner-directed. He must not derive any satisfaction from the impact of his extravagances on his "inferiors" nor from the effects on his status of his imitation of his "betters." Such a consumer in a modern setting is a rare bird indeed. The ordinary consumer certainly cannot be regarded as consistent or rational, nor can his choice be regarded as harmonious.

Indeed for a growing part of consumption in durable goods, these assumptions do not appear to be meaningful at all. Choice is intermittent, tastes change and are influenced by sales talk and are certainly not independent of the consumption of others. There is simply no reality to the sovereign consumer surveying with detachment the whole field according to his consciously, genuinely, and spontaneously felt needs. This lack of reality is further increased by the fact that, over an increasing range of goods and services, demand is largely created by the producer. The producers' advantage exists even when the things he makes, such as soap and bread, serve basic needs. In this case the fancy of the consumer is tempted toward certain brands. It is the image, the impact on other people which grows in importance, as against the satisfaction obtained by the consumption itself. Cadillacs are bought to impress, not because they represent the best means of transportation in crowded cities.

Restlessness, dissatisfaction, and ultimately unhappiness are created in order to be able to earn profit in assuaging it. A vast amount of money, in many countries larger than the total spent on education, is devoted to giving material goods an importance they ought not to have, and undermining the status quo. A European scholar graphically describes the process:

> The modern technique of developing new desires and demands is illustrated by the recent triumphal march of television in the United States. The aim of the new industry was to attract commercial sponsors who would buy time on the programs to advertise their products. To attract them, manufacturers of television sets had to induce people to equip their homes with these sets. Since little could be said about the merits of television programs, the industry has made a supreme effort to win the support of the least experienced, and least critical, consumers—the children. It has succeeded in creating a psychological climate in which the absence of a television set in a home is a humiliating stigma, not only among the middle-class families but also among some manual workers. In describing this campaign, *Life* magazine [Nov. 17, 1950, p. 26] quoted arguments used by the television industry in its newspaper copy. In one advertisement the absence of a television set in the home was characterised as an act of extreme cruelty towards children. Such negligence on the part of the parents condemned their children to social ostracism, inflicted bruises deep inside and humiliated them by forcing them to beg precious television hours from neighbours. The magazine continued with a description of spot radio announcements that tell "how little Johnnie comes home and blurts out, with sniffles, what the newspaper ads said he wouldn't tell; "I don't know what the gang's talking about any more. They all got television sets.". . . A specialist in child guidance, a children's court judge and a headmaster attested in authoritative tones that the child who doesn't have television at home is a social leper.[2]

Or, to take one more example, here is the *New Yorker* of April 21, 1951 (p. 24), quoting the *Sound Track*, a well-known U.S. trade magazine:

> Speaking of surveys, we tried an experiment the other evening. The result was not what Nimo Roper would call "significant." But it may lead you or your favorite researcher into further inquiry.
>
> To a curly-headed four year old being tucked under the covers, we posed this question: "Susie, which product brushes teeth whiter?" "Colgate, of

---

[2]W. S. and A. S. Woytinsky, *World Population and Production*, Twentieth Century Fund, p. 267.

course, Gramp." We couldn't resist another. "Which product washes clothes cleaner?" Without a moment's hesitation: "Tide." We tried once more. "Which coffee gives the best value?" When she replied "A & P and now good night Gramp," we hurried out of the child's room with other questions beating at our brain.

Brave New World? The difference between persuasion and management and information is difficult to perceive.

With the collapse of the "unassailable" and "scientific" assumption that economic values represent ultimate social values corresponding on the one hand to our personal and sovereign tastes and on the other hand to the exact value of our contribution to the sustenance of our society, the old moral basis of orthodox economics is shorn away. There remains only doubt and uncertainty.

There is, however, a more negative, more subtle, and more plausible argument in the defence of conventional economic values. This is based on the identification of freedom, democracy, peace, and free enterprise. No longer is it claimed that the individualist economic system yields the greatest increase in productive capacity, but it is argued forcibly that it is the only one compatible with freedom. This subtle change in emphasis has no doubt been the result of the acceleration of the growth of the productive capacity of the Soviet. It is the decentralization of decision-making, freedom for the individual, which now becomes the basis of the argument. As our affluence grows we can, it is said, "afford" freedom even at the cost of a slower growth of material well-being. The original argument is turned upside down, with momentous consequences.

If "freedom" is something which has to be achieved at material cost, its attractions for poor areas, which are on the verge of starvation, are far less than if freedom, as Adam Smith would have it, maximized economic prosperity and growth. Moreover the argument slides over the exact definition of what, or rather where, "freedom" is meant to be accepted as the ultimate end. To elucidate the quality of this alternative aspiration toward a worth-while ideal, we could hardly do better than to quote from a definition of free enterprise ideology in a pamphlet prepared by an American diplomat assigned to the National War College at Washington.

Faith in our democratic institutions and in their ability to meet the challenge of the modern age is high. Although some deprecate the trends towards big government and the welfare state, there is little evidence that our concepts of private property and free capitalistic enterprise have been fundamentally weakened, and much evidence that the people would bitterly resist real infringement of these concepts. Our attachment to world peace, and at the same time our readiness to fight to preserve our independence and way of life, has been amply and recently demonstrated.[3]

Thus the protection of the weak and the promotion of social security by the government is rather apologetically contrasted with the determination to maintain free capitalistic enterprise or world peace; as if these represented dangerous alternatives rather than complementing each other.

In a much similar way, the magazine *Encounter*, for instance, tried to use Sir Isaiah Berlin's celebrated inaugural lecture, *Two Concepts of Freedom*, for the same purpose. Quoting out of context a rather ambiguous footnote, it gave the impression that "economic freedom" is none other than that "minimum area of personal freedom" which, Sir Isaiah had said, must be preserved "if we are not to degrade or deny our nature." In the text of the lecture, he recognized

. . . that a frontier must be drawn between the area of private life and that of public authority. Where it is to be drawn is a *matter of argument, indeed of haggling* [my italics]. Men are largely interdependent, and no man's activity is so completely private as never to obstruct the lives of others in any way. "Freedom for the pike is death for the minnow"; the liberty of some must depend on the restraint of others. Still, a practical compromise has to be found.

The question is where the line needs to be drawn if the minnows are not to die.

But the footnote adopts a very different line. It asserts that a demand for a certain minimum of *economic* freedom—in the sense of a certain minimum command over resources—as a *necessary (though not sufficient) basis* for *personal* freedom is "a piece of political claptrap": "The Egyptian peasant needs clothes, or medicine before, and more than, personal liberty, but the minimum freedom that he needs today, and the greater degree of freedom that he may need tomorrow, is not some species of freedom peculiar to him, but identical with that of professors, artists, and millionaires." And the assertion is made:

If the liberty of myself or my class or nation depends on the misery of a vast number of other human beings, the system which promotes this is unjust and immoral. But if I curtail or lose my freedom, in order to lessen the shame of such inequality, and do not thereby materially increase the individual liberty of others, an absolute loss of liberty occurs.[4]

In this footnote Sir Isaiah appears not to differentiate between the

[3]Robert A. Fearey, *The U.S. versus the U.S.S.R.: Ideologies in Conflict*, Washington, D.C., Public Affairs Press, 1959, p. 17 (with an introduction by Paul H. Nitze, who was Dean Acheson's chief of the planning staff at the outbreak of the cold war during the Truman administration).

[4]*Two Concepts of Freedom*, Oxford, Clarendon Press, 1958, p. 11.

various spheres of human action, or to take due account of their causal interaction. He asserts that "it is nothing but a confusion of values to say that although my 'liberal,' individual freedom may go by the board, some other kind of freedom—'social' or 'economic'—is increased." Yet the very possibility of the "liberal, individual freedom" needed to preserve us from "degradation or denial of our nature" is unthinkable without *some* "economic freedom." The existence of "freedom from" depends on *some* measure of the "freedom to" which Sir Isaiah finds so dangerous and obscure a concept.

The problem of "equality" is thus inextricably intertwined with personal freedom. Economic freedom—more perhaps than other types of freedom—is in itself a combination of restraint and freedom. My freedom to dispose freely over objects implies total *restraint* on others from interfering with that freedom. In the case of "economic freedom" to dispose of *humans*, that is, slaves, it is obvious that an absolute loss of personal freedom is involved and also a loss (though not necessarily an absolute one) of economic freedom, on the part of the slave. In this case any limit to the *economic* freedom of the slave-owner—a loss of personal freedom in Sir Isaiah's terminology—would in fact represent an absolute gain of personal freedom on the part of the slave.

It was Adam Smith who said: "Civil Government, in so far as it is instituted for the protection of property is, in reality, instituted for the defence of the rich against the poor." And Tawney tellingly quotes the Final Report for the United States Commission on Industrial Relations, written in 1916: "Political freedom can exist only where there is industrial freedom. There are now within the body of our Republic industrial communities which are virtually principalities oppressive to those dependent upon them for a livelihood and a dreadful menace to the peace and welfare of the nation."[5] All this is still true, albeit less urgent in the Anglo-Saxon countries. But in the large part of the world, consisting of societies in which private property is extremely unevenly distributed, the impact of economic freedom (of the few) on personal freedom (of the many) remains much as it was in societies based on slavery. It is evidently a plain logical contradiction to call the curtailment of the absolute right to dispose of property a loss of "liberty" of the few, irrespective of whether the exercise of that liberty interferes with the individual personal liberty of the many; while denying that an increase in equality, that is, of the economic liberty of those who benefit by the curtailment, and who are thus able to make use of hitherto purely theoretical personal rights, amounts to a gain in liberty.

[5] *The Acquisitive Society*, London, 1921, p. 162.

The dialogue between a negative personal right of the individual and the ends of the community cannot be resolved on the basis of conventional economic values. We have to admit that internally the orthodox economy creates social tension because it can only achieve stability by creating unemployment in order to weaken demand and thus the position of trade unions. This tension is increased by the fact that the revival in demand, when it becomes politically necessary, is stimulated mainly by the artificial creation of new needs by increasing psychological obsolescence. If successful, this creates a sense of frustration as the satisfaction of social priorities is neglected. The richer the country, the more dangerous and embittering can be this frustration. It has been felt in the United States far more than in Britain.

Internationally the anti-inflationary policy in highly developed areas has had the effect of undermining the earning capacity of the less developed areas by reducing the demand for their products. This exacerbates the poverty, which is basically due to shortage of equipment and to the relentless acceleration of population increase caused by improved public health policies; these have reduced mortality rates without much hope of an early fall in births. Non-Communist countries, moreover, have not mobilized their vast under-employed rural manpower for productive investment. The growth of internal and international frustration belies the optimism of the original liberal economic doctrine. We must find new ways to achieve what it claimed to achieve automatically by the mysterious ways of the Hidden Hand.

This renders the task of reappraisal, which must precede that of rededication, all the more essential. Fortunately in the last year or so the two greatest offices in the non-Communist world, the Holy See and the American presidency, have been occupied by outstanding persons of deep insight and compassion, and the tide of the psychological cold war which impeded our task seems to have receded at least.

As we complete this task we shall, I believe, come to a picture of a partially planned economy in which social balance and a more equal distribution of income are sustained by a considerable public sector. Purposive education toward a less competitive, less materialistically conditioned state of existence might bring real fulfilment. Equality of opportunity, especially in education, would bring about a more equal distribution of command over resources. Stability and progress could be reconciled by a more conscious, more deliberate, and more rational way of distributing national income, and of financing the satisfaction of needs which can only be satisfied collectively. A closer supervision, indeed regulation, of the ways in which demand is influenced through advertising is another requirement. An increase in the rate of investment and economic growth in most parts of the non-Soviet orbit would seem a further precondition, as is far greater aid from the rich to the poor countries.

The dialogue between the negative personal rights of the individual and the needs of the community could at last be resolved in a general economic ease of living which would no longer depend on the uncertainty and dissatisfaction of the average man for its dynamism. Such a system would attain undisputed superiority over the totalitarian systems, which fail in their lack of regard for the dignity and integrity of the individual. Nothing less, however, is needed to match their relentless material progress.

A COMMENT

JEAN ETHIER-BLAIS

My only claim to speaking after Professor Balogh is surely that I am not an economist, but an object of Professor Balogh's scientific cogitations. And, as a reading and listening object, I find myself in agreement with his views; that is, I find his tone convincing, and therefore tend to share his outlook. However, being a Canadian, and living under the exacting orthodox economic principles of North American economists, I wonder if I do not agree with Professor Balogh to the extent only that I am not subjected to the practical effect of his theories, and that, if his thinking were implemented, I should not react against it as I do now against what he calls the conservative and financial-minded governments.

If I understand him correctly, and ignoring for a moment his trade vocabulary, the ultimate end of Professor Balogh's propositions is to evolve a social, economic, and eventually spiritual order from which Hunger and the original Fear will be banished. How can one not agree with that? In his fundamental work, *South American Meditations*, Keyserling discussed at length the dynamism of hunger and fear and demonstrated that no social thinking could progress unless it was to a large extent based on the understanding of these two vital components. When Professor Balogh concludes by saying that present trends in the opulent parts of the non-Communist world lead toward technical inferiority and spiritual weakness in the face of the Soviet challenge, he is illustrating Keyserling's intuitive perception. This brings me to my first—and brief —point. It is that in all doctrines—including the economic—there are to be found positive and negative aspects. The negative aspects can be so with regard to a sort of Ideal Reasoning, or they can be negative in themselves. If they are negative in themselves, they eventually stop the evolution of their companion positive virtues. Now for me, as a layman, this is what is most striking in capitalism, especially as we are living it today. It is essentially based on the development of personal energy directed toward profit. Thus the rational test of the capitalist spirit can be found only in the immediacy of the reward. If we look at this proposition from what could appear as an absurd angle, the negativeness of capitalist thinking is accentuated by the fact that *the desire* for this immediacy of reward is the paramount capitalist motive for action. So that the true capitalist is not necessarily Rockefeller Senior but rather the man who transforms his life into a series of unfulfilled desires, whose personal energy is constantly geared at the highest point without results. The machine goes on rotating and emits a few sparks, but it rotates in a void.

The real drama of capitalism now is not economic; it is emotional. And the basis of Professor Balogh's paper is emotional, because what is implicit in it is the contrast between a praxis which is based on Hunger and Fear and one which is based on Personal Energy and Profit. We should not deceive ourselves and think that personal energy and the profit-motive can be directed toward the common good. They cannot, except by inadvertence or as the result of outside pressures. Indeed, one should prefer the capitalist who hides his money in mattresses to the "enlightened" one; the former is logical with himself and has the strength of his negativeness; he takes his rightful place within the system; whereas the latter disguises his uncomprehensible guilt (uncomprehensible to himself) into generosity. It is one of the fundamental traits of capitalism that it should, in economic as in intellectual matters, create a culture of generosity instead of a culture of justice. This development is inherent in capitalism and is therefore *not* a contradiction of the theory; capitalism and the spirit of justice are irreconcilable terms.

Because it moves without advancing, capitalism cannot transform itself from inside. The liberal who thinks that the injection of some socialist ideals—based on justice and constant reappraisal of means—into the capitalist machinery will mobilize it, is mistaken. He is not transforming capitalism but using outside elements to keep the machine in its state of void. For example, social laws enacted by a neo-capitalist government cannot be said to be integrated into the stream of capitalist doctrine. This is why, as Professor Balogh said, the struggle against inflation is a disguised attempt to undo some of the progress toward a more even balance of power between workers and management. Any attempt to revitalize capitalism is, by nature, a temporary stop-gap; it is nothing more than a tactical retreat which, it is hoped instinctively by orthodox capitalists, will be overcome. In short, economic immobility by necessity looks backwards. It is a philosophy of regret.

Another short point. Because it is not founded on justice, the capitalist system, in order to survive both as a doctrine and consequently in fact, had to base its activities on the next best substitute which could at the same time appease its philosophical qualms and correspond to its real aspirations. That is social utilitary morality. To justify that choice of the few, which is the basis of capitalism, it had to start with the assumption that the choice was based on merit; that sin had to be punished and that there was no suffering on earth which was not well earned; and, inversely, that Grace and Success were also to be dispensed on earth. Here, in a secular context, are some of Calvin's precepts. Here also is the affiliation between the choice of the elect and economic liberalism with its tough elimination of the weak. Indeed, Calvin is the spiritual father of pragmatism, and it is not surprising that capitalism should find its directive order in Protestant countries and should have come to represent the materialistic wing of Calvin's spiritual teachings, and that, when it becomes aggressive, it should always be accompanied by democratic formalism and religious ritualistic recipes.

It is one of the merits of Professor Balogh's remarks that every sentence pushes us into reflection. I have not spoken of his admirable analysis of the psychological defense-mechanism at the basis of our rejection of the Soviet Union's economic progress. It is more challenging, in a way, because we are *living* this mechanism—which is a by-product of capitalism's capacity for refusing essential change. That immobility, I found especially dramatic—like a drifting boat, its motors dead, which is carried away by the sea, and suddenly disappears without leaving a trace.

THE REVOLUTION IN PERSONAL VALUES

ELISEO VIVAS

These remarks express the professional interest of a student of philosophy. And they are written by a man who was formed in the United States and teaches in an American university. It is in terms of his experience, with its inherent limitations, that he considers the present revolution in our values.

Let me begin with a brief indication as to how the term "value" is to be used. By value will be meant a character or aspect discerned by the mind that in appearance at least seems to be a quality or property of an object, such that attention to it elicits judgments such as: Jane is beautiful; the wine is excellent; the landscape is dull; Father Las Casas was a good man.

The values here considered are the values of the person as distinct from public or social values. And this calls for two observations. The first is that the distinction between personal and social values is one of convenience and not of kind. When values function in living—and when they do not, a man's life cannot be called human—they are never purely personal values; they are never so utterly subjective, so utterly *idiotic*, in the primitive sense of this term, as to lack altogether a social component. Nor are there social values that float above the community but are not espoused by someone at some time or other during the history of the community. The second observation is that it is important to bear in mind that the term "person" is not a descriptive but a normative category. It follows that, for technical reasons, there can be no question of reducing values by defining them in terms of value-free factors, as some philosophers claim to be able to do. Because "person" is a normative term, a mere planning for man in terms of body-comfort, in purely secularistic terms, derogates from his dignity by destroying his human dimension.*

*These matters I have discussed in my *The Moral Life and The Ethical Life*.

My basic assumption here is that values are today not only in conflict, but in a condition of radical revolution. We are undergoing the distracting and, at times, destructive effects of a revolution of major proportions. It is no mere addiction to cant that has made the word "crisis" a popular word in our language when we discuss the state of our values. It is the inevitable word. The emergence of new material conditions, the release of new forces in all domains of experience, the flood of scientific discoveries and the technological innovations that have followed them, the power realignments in the international sphere—in short, what Walter Lippmann once called "the acids of modernity," which is to say, all that has taken place since 1914, constitutes a state of affairs that we who are living through it find difficult to characterize in sober language. The upshot is a fluidity that seems to us greater than any men ever lived through in the past.

The recognition of our condition need not obscure the fact that Western history has been a succession of major crises separated by infrequent and brief periods of relative stability and harmony. The values by which our civilization has lived—the values that are our civilization—have been in a state of permanent revolution as far back as history carries us. And this appears to be the condition of all civilizations. Perhaps some Papuans and South American Indians still live in relatively static cultures with almost unchanging values as they did in the remote past. But there are not many isolated and arrested societies left in the world today. At any rate we live in a society whose values are in a state of rapid flux and radical revolution.[1]

If it does not seem necessary to argue the fact that our values are in conflict (or that they are part of the radical revolution we are undergoing), it does seem necessary to the professional student of philosophy to ask at least four, to him basic, questions:

(1) The extent and nature of the revolution.

(2) Whether values change and how the change may be interpreted when it comes about.

(3) Whether the changes that take place constitute progress or regress.

(4) The causes of the changes in our values.

[1]Some readers of Malinkowski may want to question whether the statement about primitive societies can be successfully defended. It is a matter of degree, of course, and in any case I do not mean to suggest, as writers at about the turn of the century sometimes suggested, that primitives living in custom-bound societies were not victims of conflicts of values. Relatively speaking, however, there are societies now flourishing that are practically static, and others that are in a state of vertiginous flux and serious revolution.

I shall not attempt to answer all of these questions fully. Some aspects of them fall within the province of psychologists, sociologists, political thinkers, and observers of the contemporary scene. Most of the following remarks will be confined to those aspects of the first question that come within the range of my competence, focusing chiefly on the problems of the individual.

Our value revolution is co-extensive with the whole of our experience, taken collectively and distributively, privately and publicly. It affects all men living in our world with few and negligible exceptions already alluded to. And by the world is meant the whole world, however divided by walls or curtains. The revolution is well characterized by that ugly but useful word, "global."

We tend to think of the revolution in narrower terms. We think of the awakening of the colonial peoples; at the moment of writing we are keenly aware of the fight of the American negro to gain his full citizenship and to have his dignity recognized; we think of the many conflicts that contribute to the dangerous international situation; a teacher of aesthetics or art critic may think of the revolution in art; those interested in theology may think of the challenge to belief represented by Bultmann and his movement; others think of the revolution in sex. For a cheesecloth philosopher of my acquaintance the revolution consists of an evangelistic movement he would like to lead, which consists in acknowledging the distinction between the world of everyday experience—the *Lebenswelt*—and the world to which the equations of science refer. And I know a grammarian, more silly than the philosopher, for whom the revolution has been brought to its critical point by the publication of the new Webster's. For him this catastrophic event heralds the imminent destruction of our civilization, because of the permissive linguistic habits it encourages.

But while different men, guided by different interests, may locate the heart of the revolution differently, a moment's reflection will disclose the fact that the revolution is congruous with the whole extent of our experience. Still, we may ask whether there is any form of activity today which can be taken to be moderately free from conflict. It may reveal one of the limitations of my knowledge, but I know of none. The election of Pope Paul made perfectly clear to even those of us who, like the writer, did not follow it closely, that there are conflicts in Rome. The newspapers recently have been full of the conflict between Russia and China and frequently hint about conflicts inside the Kremlin itself. There is only one sphere of activity exempt from this generalization, and only in one respect: American universities in respect to the socio-political faith of their staffs. In these seedbeds of wisdom, where Utopia flourishes at last without blemish, what academic man calls "liberalism" reigns supreme and unchallenged, nor is dissent tolerated. American professors march in serried ranks toward the socialist future with banners unfurled and eyes aglow, indifferent to the evidence from China, Russia, Scandinavia, England, moved by a faith which I can only characterize with the aid of a word recently introduced by Koestler: theirs is a sublime, struthonian faith (from *struthio*, as Koestler kindly explained for our benefit, which is Latin for ostrich). But outside of this exception—which to my mind uselessly demonstrates what is self-evident, namely that American universities are Islands of Perfection in an imperfect world—the conflict of values affects all spheres of experience and all human beings now living throughout the world, with the exception already noted of isolated, almost static, primitive societies.

Thus conceived the only picture we can envisage is one of chaos. But it seems to me that in order to do justice to the nature of the current crisis in value we must begin by acknowledging the fact of the chaos in its full extent. Not until then can we begin to reduce that chaos to some sort of order.

There is an obvious way of organizing the chaos that enables us at least to divide the task and begin the analysis. Let us think of the revolution as taking place within the individual, in his private relations to himself and to the universe, between himself and his society, and among societies. This classification is open to a number of objections, the most important of which is that, as already noted, it is one of convenience. But if we are going to get on with the job at hand we'll have to disregard these objections.

Let me begin the discussion with the observation that in spite of the tremendous gains made in our understanding of man in the last hundred years we remain incredibly naive about ourselves, as if men like Stendahl, Kierkegaard, Dostoevski, Nietzsche, and Freud (using these names literally and eponymically) had not lived. Observe, for instance, how in considering conflicts of values, we tend to think in terms of *us* and *them*: this side of the Wall and that, Liberals and Conservatives, good men and bad, friends and foes, religious men and non-believers. For many purposes, of course, this is not wrong. Only if it serves our interests is there any advantage in remembering that the Russian masters do not make up a single, monolithic party. When our representatives sit down across the table from them to discuss atomic disarmament or any other subject, or when we remember that they have gained a physical beach-head a few miles from Florida, their differences among themselves are irrelevant.

But a more accurate understanding of our situation should lead us to grasp the fact that the conflicts are internal as well as external, and that no man can live up to Santayana's ideal of the life of reason and be a harmonious man—at least not today. There are conflicts on the other side of the Wall probably fairly similar to those that we are undergoing, and there are conflicts within each and every person. It is not wrong for some purposes to say that every man is born either a Platonist or an Aristotelian, a liberal or a conservative. But the label conceals the self-divisions, the inward conflicts.

Meeting young people daily for over thirty-five years I am increasingly appalled at the amount of disorganization, inward confusion, and self-destruction with which the world is rife. And observing the few people I have known outside the campus and my colleagues—but in speaking of my colleagues I do not have in mind the present institution where I am now doing time, for my colleagues at Northwestern University are exempt from the defects of mere men—the observation is further confirmed. We think of a man as being loyal or courageous or religious. And he is. For loyalty and courage are behavioural traits, and more or less consistent behaviour is possible without disclosing the inward landscape. But if religion is more than ritual, the furnace of doubt through which Dostoevski went is one through which all religious men, I suspect, must go. Nor must we interpret Dostoevski to mean that he went through it once and came out cleansed from the impurities of doubt. His work is proof that he lived in the furnace. He had too intimate a knowledge of the Karamazovs as well as of Father Zosima to have been able to have gained it merely from objective observation. It could again be one of my limitations, but I have never known a man intimately who was free from the cracks that could lead, given untoward circumstances, to the same kind of complete split that took place in Morton Prince's Miss Beauchamp or Thigpen and Cleckley's Eve.

I do not mean that every man participates in all the phases of the revolution. He probably participates in more of them than he is aware of. But he need not be involved, at the conscious deliberate level, in each of the engagements that make up today's protracted war. Nor do I mean that the microcosm is a reflection of the macrocosm or vice versa. All that needs be asserted is that no proper understanding of the value revolution of our century can be reached unless we attend to the nature and extent of the conflicts that are taking place in each man no less than in the world.

But the word conflict does not quite do justice to the situation. Conflict there is, self-division. But ambivalence is more than conflict, and a condition of the self is a condition of ambivalence. And that does not mean that a man now hates and later loves his wife or his child, but that he hates in his loving and loves in his hating. How this is possible is difficult to make clear to oneself, given the nature of the psyche and the simplistic exigencies of logical discourse. For we have no more solved the conflict between Parmenides and Heraclitus than Plato did. The problem of change is still with us. In terms of logic the flux is unintelligible. But of course we cannot do without logic. We cannot conceive how a thing can be both A and non-A in the same sense at the same time. But ambivalence is precisely that and no less, or I have totally misread Dostoevski and Freud. And here my language betrays me, for if that is what ambivalence is, it cannot be precisely both things at once. It can only be both in the most unprecise and obscure sense.

It does not follow from these remarks that the life of reason is an utterly useless dream. It must remain the goal toward which we must aspire if we are to retain a firm hold on our humanity. But it is a goal toward which we shall make poor progress if we are ignorant of the difficulties involved in reaching it. The defenders of reason often overlook the fact that one way to discredit reason is to misrepresent it. One of the urgent jobs philosophers have to undertake today is not that of defending reason, but of redefining reason in view of all that has happened since the shallow and purblind age of the Enlightenment.

One more observation is called for. I may have given the impression that I believe that conflict is, without qualification, undesirable. That would be the case only if the primary value, to which all other values had to yield pride of place, were stasis. But that is not the case with our civilization. Some conflicts are to be welcomed because they are creative of needed change. One of the conflicts, of course, among us, and within us, is as to how much and in what direction and in respect to what areas of experience change is desirable. But no one—no one in his right mind today, that is—can wish to arrest the process of history. In any case it is not possible: as soon order the tides to stop.

This is all that can be said in general terms about the revolution of values at the individual level. We must turn to the consideration of more specific matters. But rather than undertake an enumeration of what seems to me to be the most important areas of conflict—which would be no more than specification of the important facets of individual activity today—I shall take up two conflicts which happen to interest me. I shall turn first to the problems that arose when we were forced to face the question of man's nature upon the publication of *The Origin of the Species*. In the last hundred years we have had to revise thoroughly our views of our own nature. No more than positive science began with Galileo or Copernicus, did the revision to which I refer begin with Darwin or was it forced on us solely by advances in the field of biology. But 1859 is a good, although arbitrary date from which to begin our considerations.

The story is well known as to how the publication of Darwin's book began a war which, again arbitrarily, may be said to have come to an end in the pathetic comedy enacted in the court-room of Dayton, Tennessee. We can, therefore, plunge right into our problem by asking: what did the publication of *The Origin* do? From the philosophical point of view it constituted an enormous enlargement in breadth and depth of our knowledge of ourselves and our proper place in nature. The qualifications that have to be made for this statement to meet the exigencies of accuracy do not force its withdrawal. *The Origin* put positive knowledge as regards man's relationship to nature in place of purely philosophical speculations or of mythic accounts of his origin. The qualification that has to be introduced is that it allowed a great deal of mere speculation to be smuggled in with the positive knowledge. It led to uncritical extrapolation from biology to culture. But the kind of knowledge we have of man's biological origin simply is not matched by the speculative theories as to his cultural origin. A few chipped stones and evidence of human skeletons that were ritually buried tell us nothing of the origin of language, the origin of morality, religion, art. And the contention that acceptance of the theory of evolution makes it impossible for us to believe in Genesis in the way in which Bishop Wilberforce and his contemporaries believed in it—as it does—is a psychological explanation, not an argument.

Whatever the merit of this qualification, it cannot be denied that while enlarging and basing on solid ground our knowledge of man's relation to nature, evolution brought about a profound dislocation and philosophical problems of major magnitude, all of which affect us, whether we are aware of it or not, both practically and theoretically. Because in academic circles we accept as a matter of course the primacy of knowledge over all other values, as a necessary postulate of our professional life, we tend to overlook the nature of some of the problems that *The Origin* brought in its train.[2]

I do not have in mind solely its impact on religion, although that has

[2]Professor Giovanni Sartori has called my attention to the fact that Darwin had no influence on continental philosophy but solely on English and American thought. If the statement is true, it constitutes a serious indictment of the men who were not challenged by *The Origin*. But is it true? Nietzsche may be dismissed by academic philosophers—I would not dismiss him. But can Bergson?

been serious enough. The warfare between science and religion, as it has been called, has been the subject of much study and in general terms at least, we are all fairly conversant with the history of the conflict: the campaigns and engagements that have occurred, and the armistices and settlements by which mediators at various times have sought to put an end to the hostilities. I am thinking of the impact of evolution in other areas, an impact that has caused as profound a dislocation as it caused on religion although perhaps not as dramatic or even as obvious. Nor am I thinking of Darwin's direct and explicit influence on philosophers, broad and deep as it was. I am thinking rather of the challenge that his thought constituted or should have constituted for thinkers, whether academic or not, and of the manner in which directly and indirectly he changed the intellectual climate of thought.

Let us consider briefly two predicaments forced on us at the intellectual level by evolution which have had serious influence on our values. The first of these is the corrosive effect that it has had on the belief in ontic structures. By the term "ontic structures" I mean such objects of thought as the habits of nature, as embodied in the laws of science, and the value universals over the interpretation of which moral philosophers have been disputing for two millennia. These objects of protracted dispute were taken by Plato and many thinkers since his day to have some sort of status in being, some sort of reality. But that they have any other kind of reality but that which can be claimed for a generalization has been denied by a majority of contemporary Anglo-American philosophers. These men are nominalists. The acceptance of nominalism is not solely the effect of the spread of evolution. In the history of ideas nothing is simple. But the rejection of the notion of fixed species has added its influence to the inability of most educated men to believe that reality is objectively structured.

But why is this important? It is important in itself, in a purely philosophical sense, since it presents philosophers with a multitude of puzzles that cannot be left unsolved. For instance: if there are no structures, if particulars constitute the only reality and universals are only generalizations in discourse, what does the scientist discover when he discovers the laws of nature? The invariant relations that are the objects of his search seem to be more than his own formulations, the formulations seem to refer to something which somehow is part of the aspect of nature he studies. But how are we to interpret that to which the formulations refer if reality is nothing but particulars and the structures are only generalizations?

Serious as are the purely intellectual consequences of nominalism, I do not deem them lamentable, for a serious thinker is not dismayed by problems: he is challenged by them. But nominalism also leads to important practical consequences and these are disastrous. Consider one of them. Nominalism is one of the sources of our facile value relativism. The slogan with which we seriously meet the request for the procedures and criteria for the criticism of moral judgments is, "There are no absolutes." Apparently there is one, for the tone with which the dictum is uttered brooks no challenge. The answer to the dictum is that as regards so hopelessly polysemic a term as the term "absolute," in some of its meanings there certainly are not. But in other senses, it is less than absolutely certain whether there are or not.

In any case our complacent dismissal, not only of absolutes, whatever that be, but of all ontic structures, denies us the basis for objective criticism of value judgments and the basis for the moral resolution of radical moral conflicts. This would have no disastrous consequences if we were living in a stable society and if we could therefore depend on fairly well defined mores for the resolution of our moral perplexities and conflicts. But we have no such recourse. There are no old men of the tribe, and those on whom we would thrust the honour know no more what ought to be done than the rest of us.

It should be noted that the relationship between evolution and nominalism is not a relationship of implication but a relationship of entailment. It could have happened differently. But given the climate of opinion in which Darwin's hypothesis exploded, given the ruthless erosion of modern man's capacity to believe in structures that is the heritage of modern empiricism, and given the effect of many other factors, evolution made its mighty contribution to the regnant conviction: value judgments have no objective referend; there are no absolutes. This is one of the unarguable articles of faith of the majority of our contemporary philosophers.

Another result of evolution was its denial of the basis on which, prior to 1859, we grounded our respect for man. Here again I must be permitted to reiterate that nothing in the history of ideas is simple. But certainly, and at least before the adjustment took place and the acceptance of the Darwinian hypothesis became universal (as it is today among the educated), the ground for our respect for man was his unique place in nature. When His Lordship, Samuel Wilberforce, the Bishop of Oxford—better known to his contemporaries under the unenviable moniker of Soapy Sam—put his famous question to Darwin's Bulldog, this eminent clergyman exposed his ignorance of evolution in a pitiful manner. But a century after Darwin we have no right to overlook, as

Darwin's friends in their anger understandably did, that Samivel, as Huxley called his clerical antagonist, was by the form of his ill-conceived wit expressing, among other things, his concern for man's dignity.

But what do I mean by the reference to a pathetic exhibition by a clever yet ignorant man of a hundred years ago? What does the story have to do with the value of conflicts of men today? Let me answer this question in concrete terms. If the revolt against colonialism that we have witnessed and the fight of the American negro against inequality are, as I imagine we all take them to be, more than a passing historical incident, if they represent a major turning point in the history of our contemporary civilization, the movement comes at a time when the theoretical basis for our belief has been swept away, along with Wilberforce's faith and much else. Now, those of us who believe in the justice of the demand —for the others have only the problem of how to reject it successfully— if we claim to be philosophically responsible, are called upon to exhibit the ground for our belief. Take seriously that challenge and you are forced, I submit, to put in question the regnant orthodoxy of Anglo-American philosophy in our age.

But let us not make a mistake as to what is demanded of us. It is not proof of *de facto* equality, a claim easily shown up for what it is, utterly without ground. Nor for the equality of capacities, the potential equality in which the anthropologists insist. What we must exhibit is the ground for the obligation of each man to treat others with unqualified respect irrespective of their potential or actualized equality or capacities. The obligation, therefore, cannot be based on the contention of contemporary anthropology that there are no differences in capacities among men or among the peoples of the world. The equality of capacities is irrelevant, and not because differences may or may not exist, but because if the differences exist, whether they favour the Negritos, the Pygmies, or the white of Toronto or Chicago, they have no bearing whatever on the question. They do not define the respect one man owes another. At best they can have a bearing only on the behavioural manner in which that respect will be manifested. And this holds whatever superiorities or inferiorities, actual or potential, may be found among peoples or individuals. The respect one individual owes another has nothing to do with the colour of the skin, the shape of the nose, the slant of the eyes, the IQ however measured, or, for that matter, whether he is a good man or evil. Deny this seriously, push the denial to the logical extreme, as fortunately it is seldom possible to do in actuality, and you end up with the systematic elimination of those that the bureaucrat in cahoots with the technical expert decides to eliminate: those declared to be sub-human, and those marked as the unfit by the bleeding hearts of the agents of the top commissar.

What is urgently needed, in short, is a philosophical ground for our conviction. If it cannot be furnished outside a theological or a metaphysical perspective, and if these perspectives are inadmissible, as many of the regnant academic philosophies take them to be, the conviction must be given up. If it cannot be given up, these perspectives deserve careful and scrupulously fair re-examination.

The conflict of value for the individual that I have just discussed is that generated by the impact of evolution on the traditional ethos in the midst of which Darwin's book exploded in 1859. Let us turn to another conflict.

If you turn to the last paragraph of the eighteenth lecture of Freud's *A General Introduction to Psychoanalysis*, you will read that humanity in the course of history "has endured three great outrages from the hands of science." The first from Copernicus, the second from Darwin and Wallace, and the third from psychoanalysis. This last outrage, Freud tells us, is the most bitter of all. For "psychoanalysis is endeavoring to prove that the 'ego' of each one of us is not even master in his own house, but must remain content with the veriest scraps of information about what is going on unconsciously in his own mind." It would not be difficult to show that Freud's simplification of the history of ideas overlooked other thinkers that outraged man's self-esteem or shook violently the foundations of his sustaining faith: one thinks of Nietzsche, of course, and of Marx. But Freud was writing in a specific context. Moreover, Freud was perfectly well aware that the outrage inflicted by psychoanalysis is not defined exhaustively in the narrow terms in which he defined it. His pan-sexuality, his insistence that respectability covered a sluggish, malodorous cleaca, his denial of the clean-cut distinction between sanity and insanity, his determinism, his hedonism, his unerring capacity to come up always with an explanation of behaviour which demeans human self-esteem, the hard, pitiless glare of his rationalism, withering and bleaching the romantic illusions it fell on—these and many other components of his theory have been for many of his readers the causes of the deep outrage.

But just as there would have been no conflict in the case of Darwin, had his hypothesis not possessed at least *prima facie* authority, so there would have been no outrage if Freud had been, as many of us would still like to believe, an intellectual clown possessed of a fantastic if deranged imagination, making out of whole cloth a theory of human nature that had no relation whatever to the reality it pretended to be about. Psychoanalysis inflicts an outrage because it constitutes an immense enlargement and deepening of our knowledge of man. For that reason it is desirable to consider first what I take to be the nature and importance of Freud's contribution.

Freudian theory has been confronted with two serious challenges. The effectiveness of its therapeutic technique has been questioned and the scientific nature of its hypotheses has been denied. An examination of claims and counterclaims in these respects is most important, but I shall not enter into such an examination. I shall consider Freud as a philosophical anthropologist *or* as a philosopher of culture—and let me stress the "or," because I take the two disciplines to be one and the same when properly understood. Whether or not there is positive evidence that his technique of therapy is effective, whether he is a scientist or not, in the usual meaning of the word, he has deepened and broadened our perspective of man and of culture. We knew in general terms before Lancelot Law Whyte's recent *The Unconcious Before Freud* that the notion of the unconscious was no *ex nihilo* invention of the father of psychoanalysis. But although an exaggeration, it is not altogether unfair to say that Freud added a third dimension to our conception of man. The notion of the unconscious began to play the role it plays today because of the way he elaborated it, anchored it in clinical data, and went on to apply it to our cultural institutions. I say "he anchored it," thus putting it vaguely, because I want to avoid saying that he furnished verifiable evidence, since the claim would force me to examine one of the criticisms I have decided to bypass.

Jerome Bruner ends an elegant little essay on Freud with an eloquent paragraph a couple of lines of which read as follows: "Freud's mode of thought is not a theory in the conventional sense, it is a metaphor, an analogy, a way of conceiving man, a drama."[3] This is the kind of phrase that lends itself all too readily to quotation, but will lead us to undervalue Freud's contribution if we overlook—as Bruner does not—the impact of Freud on the thought of his day. Put aside the physical sciences and there is no discipline that has not felt the impact of Freud. The fact is too well known to require detailed specification. Freud has opened new areas of inquiry and forced the redirection of old ones. He has shown that old mythologies were not sheer inventions. Consider only the impact he has had on anthropology and on literary criticism. The influence of Freud on these disciplines cannot be exaggerated. Or consider how his view of man "confirms" the myth of original sin. The

---

[3]Jerome Bruner, "Freud and the Image of Man," in *Freud and the Twentieth Century*. Ed. Benjamin Nelson, N.Y., Meridian Books Inc., 1957, p. 285.

mind of anyone taking Freud seriously is thoroughly altered, deepened, broadened. He cannot enter the Freudian universe, immerse himself in it fully, and come out as he went in. His vision is altered, it gains in acuity. For him human experience acquires a depth it lacked before, it acquires a resonance to which other writers had been adding—Dostoevski, Nietzsche, Stendahl, the thinkers studied by Whyte. On our knowledge of man Freud impresses the stamp of his genius.

Asked to be more specific about the nature of Freud's contribution, I would state it as follows. Having added a third dimension to our conception of man, having probed the depths of the psyche as only the poets before him did, he has enabled us to grasp in a firm manner we could not have achieved earlier, the unity of human culture and the basic cracks inherent in it. Let us consider first the unity. He exhibits it because the pan-sexuality he posits at its basis suggests, by pointing specifically with dazzling ingenuity to its connections, how the heterogeneous conscious activities of man could have their unifying source in some such principle as Eros.

Let me illustrate. (And I am certain that the autobiographical impertinence of the illustration will be forgiven me for the sake of the light it will throw on the meaning I am trying to present.) Indian sculpture remains a puzzle to Western eyes until the viewer has immersed himself in Freud. At least that was one man's experience. In Western art sensuality is sensuality and spirituality is spirituality. Renoir and El Greco are poles apart. The Venetians and Byzantine icon painters turn their faces to opposite quarters. The poetry of San Juan de la Cruz—the blatant eroticism in the service of expressing transcendent longing and pure spiritual consummation—we take without understanding or puzzling. He is a mystic, and with the term we manage to cover much mystery. But Indian sculpture is a blending of animality and spirituality which, because we come upon it as aliens, sets up a problem for us. We are disturbed by the peregrine denial of what we have always taken to be separate and beyond union. In our Western experience we have frequently found these two mixed. Here they are in synthesis. What is before our eyes is deeply disturbing—and attractive in its repulsiveness. But consider it from the Freudian perspective and it is no longer puzzling, since the spirit (unless we hang, for dear life, on to some sort of metaphysical dualism such as Descartes'), whatever its ultimate status in being, is in us, animals that we are, deeply rooted in, and fed by, the flesh. It may be argued that the same would follow from other philosophies; indeed, a thoroughgoing monistic materialism would have less difficulty than Freud's hesitant dualism of principles. And in theory this point must be conceded. But I know of no other contemporary philosophy that attempts to give as detailed a genetic account of the development of man's cultural manifestations as Freud's. I do not mean that he solved these problems. All he did was force them on our attention in such a way that we had to ask the questions properly. It is because what he touched he changed or reactivated, and because he opened so many utterly unsuspected vistas, that we must apply to him a term much abused since Whitehead first used it: Freud was one of the very few genuinely seminal thinkers of the first half of our century. And that is enough for a serious student of philosophy to expect from a thinker. But let me stress the term contemporary and let me make explicit what I mean by it. For there are many philosophies flourishing today that are chronologically contemporary; but it is erroneous to call them contemporary if by the term be meant a philosophy that faces the full range of today's experience. Philosophies that have an animus against the positive sciences—as do some of the *Lebenswelt* philosophies that are at the moment screaming for attention—are not contemporary; they are hopelessly reactionary.

But Freud is a difficult man, and he never lets us off easily. Having led us to appreciate, as we didn't before, the unity of flesh and spirit, he enjoys our discomfiture when he points out that the institutions of man are flawed through and through. Civilization breeds ineradicable discontent. The child's love is instinct with hatred of his father and desire for the possession of his mother. Aggressiveness or the desire to suffer actual physical pain is rife in love. God? Ah, he is the image of the father, blown up and projected into the blue; but remember that the father we never truly loved, for we were his rivals and lived in fear he would castrate us. Take any nucleus of cultural activity that has some sort of identifiable autonomy and two observations are true of it. If it has been taken to be a lily, remember that it grows in a dung pile; if it has been taken to be the source of satisfaction, you will soon observe in those who derive satisfaction from it neurotic traits that bespeak the ambivalence it generates.

At this point you want to know whether a system that is a tangle of clinical observation of great acuity, insights of genius, speculative freewheeling, and serious error—as I take it to be—is, in my opinion, the new evangel for our day. No, I do not think it is. Keeping within the context of our topic—because from a different standpoint a different judgment would have to be hazarded—the value of Freud's contribution consists in the fact that he identified some of the most serious of the value conflicts we are undergoing and suggested where we could go for light on their causes. When we take him seriously we find ourselves agreeing with him at least this much: that where he tells us to look for the source of our difficulties, there undoubtedly those sources at least in part are to be found. And with that realization the Pelagian optimism that is deeply instinct in us is bleached off. A man can call himself a liberal—in the American acceptance of the term—and claim at the same time that he takes Freud seriously, only if he is endowed with the usual capacity men are endowed with for entertaining contradictions in their capacious minds. While therefore I would not claim that Freud brings us the whole truth—no philosopher ever performed that feat—I do claim that his theories are immensely relevant to us. But more, they must contain some truth or they would not leave us, upon our becoming acquainted with them, with a sense of enlarged vision. Whatever the future may have in store for his ideas, for us, living in the middle of the twentieth century, Freud is still an event of major importance.

This claim I would make for Freud in spite of serious errors in his thought of which I am aware. I shall mention in a summary fashion a number of them that seem to me of capital importance. But let me say first that if the discovery of error totally invalidated a philosophy, all philosophical systems would be utterly useless. The most serious and certainly one of the most pervasive of Freud's errors is the way in which he commits systematically the genetic fallacy. God is nothing but . . . art is nothing but . . . the conscience is nothing but. . . . Setting off on a genetic enquiry, the late nineteenth-century village atheist, who is one of the selves that made up his psyche, takes over and reduces whatever is the object of inquiry to something else. He would not admit that there may be objective components whose discovery may have been made possible by the operation of subjective factors. Thus, while our need for something to take the place of the comforting father may be one of the factors that lead us to the discovery of God, He is more than the need. And thus again, while the pattern of espoused values is unquestionably determined by parental influence, it is more than the prohibitions and permissions that constituted part of our early training. And thus again, while it would take abysmal obtuseness or colossal prudery to deny that sex is an important component in our aesthetic activity, Freud himself had the good sense to remind us that before the mystery of creativity, psychoanalysis is impotent.

Another of the pervasive errors of Freud is his coarse hedonism. Working with an instinct psychology, Freud assumes that instincts or drives seek pleasure. But what an instinct seeks is completion of a state of affairs, satisfaction: hunger seeks food; thirst, water; sex, discharge through the appropriate object. The satisfaction normally produces pleasure, and upon the enjoyment of it it is thereafter prospectively envisaged as part of the state of affairs that the satisfaction of the drive will bring about. The coarse hedonism and the reductionism encourage a down-grading of the aspirations and efforts of man.

A third criticism to which the Freudian philosophy is open is its uncompromising determinism. Freud leaves no room for spontaneity or creativity. And this condemns many of his best insights to unnecessary error. One of his great contributions (as I have already intimated) is the suggestions he has made about the genetic factors of culture. This is a problem that contemporary naturalistic philosophers, incapable of handling it in their terms, try to cover up with fig-leaf words like "emergence," terms that explain nothing and obfuscate the issue. Freud attacks this problem frontally. But he condemns his efforts to failure from the start by seeking a solution with a cast-iron determinism which is one of the worst aspects of his nineteenth-century patrimony.

Freud has been criticized not only because of his intellectual errors but because of the bad consequences that his theories have let loose in our distracted world. He has been blamed for the sexual revolution that is taking place today. But no one man could bring about an event of such a complex nature. And because of his determinism and his complex analysis of the neurotic psyche, he has been charged with encouraging irresponsibility. If our inability to carry on normally—it is said that he argues—is the result of illness and not of moral turpitude, we cannot help being what we are. I would not question that some readers of Freud have misused him in this manner. But the fault is not Freud's but that of those who misinterpret him.

In spite of all the errors that may detract from the value of his insight, and they are not few, we cannot dismiss him. Of course some do. But those who do, dismiss him out of a depth of intellectual irresponsibility that arises from intransigent partisanship. Today, however, we need no longer be concerned with his detractors. As the sun of history shifts, the shadow of this severe man may grow larger or smaller. Today it falls over our civilization, and we can avoid it only by closing our eyes.

Let me note again, before taking up the second of my original questions, that I shall deal with it and the two following questions only in the briefest manner possible.

That in a dynamic society values are in a state of constant change is a tautology. That they do not all change in the same manner and at the same rate is a truism. Some are destroyed, some lose their allure, new ones are discovered and are somehow integrated into the operative pattern of culture. But there is one type of change that deserves attention in view of our problem. What we take to be a change in value is often a change in the manner of its manifestation. For the same value may be embodied in different material vehicles or behavioural modes of expression.

The meaning of the distinction is easily grasped with the aid of an illustration. Consider the well-known story told by Herodotus in the third book of the *History* from which value relativists have wrongly derived so much comfort. Darius asks certain Greeks and Callatians how much he would have to pay them, for the Greeks to eat, and the Callatians to burn, their fathers upon their death. Of course both are outraged by the thought. A Greek burns his father as is proper, and a Callatian eats him. Note that what the story illustrates is cultural pluralism, not cultural relativism. It is true that the two acts differ, but the same idea or form is inherent in or in-forms each. Both are means of expressing filial piety toward a dead father.

For convenience let me introduce a verbal distinction between a concrete value and the value-idea that in-forms it. Many value conflicts arise from intolerance toward concrete values that are in-formed by the same idea that in-forms our values. These conflicts may be as costly as conflicts between values in-formed by incompatible value-ideas, as the wars of religion among Christians show. But there seems to be less rational justification for these conflicts than there is for conflicts about concrete values embodying incompatible value-ideas. Nor does the recognition that a custom different from our own expresses the same value-idea need to weaken our attachment to the concrete values we espouse. Let Callatians eat their fathers if that is how they prefer to express their filial piety. They have their customs and we have ours. It would take more than a generation, no doubt, to teach Greeks to behave as proper Callatians. But we shall have a better grasp of the devastation that value conflicts often bring with them, and will gain a better estimate of our intolerance, if we remember the distinction I have suggested.

What I have called the idea in-forming a concrete value, anthropologists call a value universal, and at least one of them, Clyde Kluckhohn, undertook the search for them in the hope of avoiding some of the disastrous consequences of value relativism which social scientists seem to be sworn to uphold. But it must be observed that their nominalism and their repudiation of teleology condemns their efforts to futility in advance. They interpret a value universal as a generalization from particulars which applies to any given particular only in so far as it happens to resemble the particulars from which the generalization was drawn. Such a universal is merely descriptive and cannot play a normative role.

The question as to whether the changes that are taking place in our value schemes are to be interpreted as progress or regression is extremely difficult for the professional student of philosophy because of the technical problems that have to be disposed of before he can assert the possibility of rational choice among values.

But let us bypass these technical puzzles, and call attention to a paradox that confronts us and that constitutes, in my view, a genuine threat for the future.

Most of us would agree, I have no doubt, that the social revolution taking place in the world has the sympathy of all those who are genuinely concerned with the right of the individual to the opportunity to develop his individuality to the full. It is our concern for the individual that justifies our impatience with those who in any way would deny the desirability of extending the advantages of our civilization to those to whom the advantages have until now been denied. But a man endowed with a sense of responsibility toward the full human being and with a capacity for piety toward his civilization qualifies the expression of his sympathy with care. Thus, ultimately, between the socialist planner and the man with a sense of responsibility the difference lies in their opposite conceptions of human excellence. The socialist wants nothing more than a well-fed animal. Or at least that is as far as his words go. For back of his claims, back of his bleeding heart and his demagogic statistics, back of his scientistic demonstrations, his soap-box eloquence, it is easy to see the brutal arrogance and the relentless drive for power. He is quite ready to plan our life away—for the good of man as he sees it. But who is this man whose good he wants? An abstract man, a figment of his own imagination, a rationalization to enable him to put his hands on the controls. He'll push us here and there, into communes; he'll order us off into the bush, to work with our hands. With his scientistic pseudo-knowledge he'll turn us all into a herd, and he'll proceed to tell us where we can pasture and when and for how long, where we can rest, where and when we can sleep and with whom—all for the benefit of man and for the sake of the satisfaction of his own arrogant lust for power. Oh yes, he'll feed us well—*mañana*, after the next five-year plan succeeds. In the meantime we have to work for the socialist future. Of course he believes in co-operation, this bleeding heart; but he believes in a special kind of co-operation, for you must not expect him to be simple-minded. The co-operation he believes in is that defined by a cynical old dean under whom I once had the misfortune to serve, who used to define and practice co-operation as the process whereby you cooped while he operated.

But don't be deceived; these lovers of abstract man are the architects of the already dawning *Brave New World*. Which means that the abstract blueprint of man is turning into a concrete reality. And remember that what makes this ugly dystopia the threat that it is is not the gadgets, nor the facile sex, nor the controlled escape from reality, nor the displacement of God and of tragedy, nor the ingenious gimmicks incorporated by Huxley into his picture. These are props. At the heart of the picture are two factors: the discretionary control by an utterly rational Big Wheel, Mustapha Mond, a benevolent Big Brother, and the institutionalization of purely "rational" values of a secular nature. The dystopia consists in the realization of Bentham's dream. It is an old, old story. But men, desperate in their frustrations, will fall again, as they have in the past, for the bleeding heart and the crocodile tears that promise them a full belly.

Am I dreaming nightmares in full daylight? If you are a secularist and a socialist you must think I am. But why don't you really consider the matter? In our concern for our own body comfort and for the body comfort of all the inhabitants of the earth we are drifting into a state of affairs that, allowed to continue to its logical conclusion, will end by denying the individual all freedom to be himself in his own way. The growth of the welfare state will produce what Louis Baudin (in a book that ought to be read by anyone concerned with the future of man, *A Socialist State: The Incas of Peru*) has called "a menagerie of happy men." For as the state broadens the scope of its activities it increases its power. But broaden them it must, for the technological complexities of our world can only be managed by experts. But the state is not a physical entity. As the sheep encounter it, the state is someone behind a desk interpreting the rule book, and back of him the writer of the rules, the expert, armed with discretionary power. I do not know how far government by bureaucratic commissions has proliferated in Canada, but anyone interested in the individual's personal freedom ought to read Lowell Mason's *The Language of Dissent*, to get a view of how far bureaucracy has developed in the United States and what that development means. Bureaucracy expands and as it does the power-thirsty bureaucrat strengthens his grip over all the sub-classes of citizens in the state. Men, always for their own good of course, as laid down by the planners, slowly lose their discretionary freedom. And gradually, apparently without premeditation or intent on the part of anyone—for the arrogance and the will to power of the expert is concealed behind the statistics and the cajolery of the bleeding heart—the merely unpleasant menagerie of happy men turns into the horror of the *Brave New World*. The expert behind the man behind the desk tells the citizen what he is permitted to desire. But the latter suffers no regret since he suffers no deprivation. The bleeding heart who rules in the paternal state gently but ruthlessly conditions him not to desire what he cannot get.

Developments in history are not inevitable and historical predictions are for the most part silly. But the condition of mankind envisaged by Dostoevski in his poem of "The Grand Inquisitor," of which Huxley's dystopia is an up-to-date version, is not an impossible development. It apparently flowered fully in the thoroughly Benthamite empire of the Incas. It is already a shoot that has broken the soil of our world. And some of the reports we have from Sweden where welfarism is advanced do not make pleasant reading. But being somewhat pessimistic about the future, I leave these unpleasant cavils aside to turn to the last question.

A responsible discussion of the causes of the revolution in our values must be prefaced by the observation that I have radical scruples as to the use of the cause-effect category in the interpretation of history.

But if we allow the use of this category, it seems to me that the best organization of the phenomena that can be made would indicate that the revolution is "the effect" of the change in our Western civilization from a dominantly sacramental culture into an increasingly secular one, and that this change has been brought about in turn by the accelerating development of the positive sciences and the technological improvements that they have made possible. Thus, another paradox emerges—at least for some of us. For the total secularization of society cannot be, for any responsible person who has thought about these matters, a desirable state of affairs. But it seems to be another of the goals toward which we are moving.

I do not draw from these observations an unqualified pessimistic conclusion. While I have a deep-rooted fear that Western man is in the grip of a death-wish that may lead him to destruction—Khrushchev may be right: they may yet bury us—I am keenly aware of the fact that the challenges we are confronted with make our lives worth living if arduous. One man at least finds it difficult to conceive of another age in which it would have been more challenging to live. True, the all-controlling state ruled by a Caesar who is in turn ruled by the planners seems imminent. But it has not yet gained the stranglehold it aims for. Man is an unpredictable animal. He may yet revolt against the Caesars and the planners with the bleeding hearts and the cold lust for power who control the Caesars.

ON PERSONAL MORAL VALUES

JEAN ETHIER-BLAIS

The essential conflict in life is between man and Mankind. It becomes, at times, an almost unbearable contradiction. We live in a society the avowed aim of which is not only to permit, but to accelerate, personal development; and yet, there have existed few societies which have insisted more on conformity, that is, subservience of the individual to a pattern of conduct set by the anonymous mass. At the same time that we are inwardly exalted by the limitless possibilities in the search for, and flowering, of self, we are restrained by the amorphous conservatism, with regard to spiritual and intellectual values, of the superficially evolved mass which surrounds us. Not that this is not a natural phenomenon; it seems to be a law of nature that spiritual extinction is the necessary corollary of any mass development. And by "spiritual extinction" I do not mean the immediate disappearance of spiritual (or moral) patterns. By "extinction" I mean ossification.

Society will stick by its set of values; it will refuse to budge; it will consider all spiritual and moral values, apart from its static own, as false and debilitating. Its primary aim will never be to evolve better standards, but to sit back and enjoy those it already has. In these circumstances, any change becomes revolutionary. A morally and spiritually satiated society invites drastic new beginnings; it needs, as it were, to be purged. The very spectacle of its mass conservatism is bound to bring about a violent reaction.

The moral values we live on, our Christianity, our medieval justice, our hedonistic egotism, are never questioned. Indeed, we are living in a hypocritical world; as Stephan Zweig wrote:

What is insisted upon is no longer a moral state of being, but merely a moral type of behaviour, each man having to live as if he were motivated by respect for the interests of others. How far, in this behaviour, the conduct of the individual is truly moral in the spiritual sense of the term, remains his own private affair; and all he need guard against is being detected in any breach of the moral code.

When, at the crossroads, man chose "behaviour" instead of "being," what he in fact did, was to prefer mechanistic rituals to spirituality. Rituals are appearances and it is in the nature of appearances, once they have assumed the figure of reality, to transform this very reality, of which they are but the ridiculous opposite, into absurdity. This is one of the reasons why all attempts to reach for spirituality are matter-of-factly considered as part of an esoteric process. The function of the jester is to revile the king; but there is no example of a king who has suffered in his kingship from histrionic irony. In this wise, ritual cannot challenge spiritually; for the few, it enhances its necessity. And, whatever its efforts, ritual cannot grasp man in its entirety; it can analyse its deportment, it can put its behaviour on file; it cannot comprehend him. In such, our behaviourist context, it is natural that man should have been considered, and still is, as an object of science, not of intuitive understanding. . . . The "moral type of behaviour" has led to a sort of disaffection for the study of man and to an irrepressible urge to study the mass.

What complicates the moral contradiction inherent in such a state of affairs is the fact that there exists in every man, even the greatest, a natural tendency to become part of the stagnant mass, an unidentified numeral, indescribable like Humanity itself; and yet, by a single movement of the mind, at the same time that man wishes to disappear into dire anonymity, he is impatient with the limits set by this same mass to the nature and scope of his personal development. It is impossible to strike a balance here; to disappear and shine at the same time, to be engulfed and yet to remain singular. "Stirb und Werde," writes Goethe. But this is romanticism; what we instinctively desire is not to die in order to be re-born, or just to be, but to flower naturally, unhindered by the development outside us, for centuries, of conventions and laws, applicable to the mass, but not to us. It is not a matter of "aristocratic" against "vulgar" minds. It is a natural tendency in man. To transcend, to rise above anonymous excellence. There is, in Chartres Cathedral, a sculpture which represents Adam in the very process of being created. He is gushing out of the stone, pushed into being by God; and one can feel, in the expression of pain and joy which is Adam's at that particular moment, that he is not Adam alone, but also the image of God who is creating him. There is also surprise on that first of faces; surprise and questioning. As if Adam realized that not only is he a man, but already more or less than himself, as the case may be, the Image of something else. I am not myself, from the very first gasp, I am not myself, cries man—if I have, throughout life, to remain the Image of Someone whose existence I can contest, but whose presence, in spite of myself, through centuries of pressure, I feel! Does the conflict not become twofold if man, in order to take possession of himself, has to wage war against God and Humanity?

It is in this conflict that personal moral values are to be found. Essentially, they are the image of the individual's inability to resolve in a positive way his relations with God and the passive development of mankind as a whole. It is evident, in this context, that there exist only two possible ways out of this moral dilemma: either to dismiss the problem entirely and accept the canons of morality which have come down to us; or, while pretending that one accepts them, to write, in the secret of one's heart and mind, a new grammar of conduct, if not entirely different in its workings from the accepted one, at least different in its relation to one's sensibility. The tragedy of acceptance is that one will, in fact, give up one's fundamental right to judge what is right and what is wrong. In other words, one automatically accepts the supremacy of the police code. Whether or not we are prepared to admit it, most of us live according to that code, and to that code only. We therefore live in a universe where fear and anguish are at the very basis of our moral determination. It is a religious code, in the sense that it is formally and historically imbricated in the evolution of religious thinking. But, on the other hand, it is profoundly anti-religious since it rejects the moral dialogue which should precede its acceptance. We accept it atavistically; our gesture is automatic, like the woman in the Wasteland, who "smooths her hair with automatic hand." We refuse to take a stand. Here again Society triumphs over the thinking individual, not by reasoning with him, but by forcing him to adopt blindly a moral structure which is not necessarily the one he would have chosen himself, had he been free.

And yet, we deify the gangster, the harlot, and the assassin; we feel a sneaking respect for those who break the laws, not because we approve of their crimes, but only in so far as they "break the law," as if crime, in its very essence, were the only gap left for effective protest. In that sense, the criminal represents and symbolizes us in truer fashion than does the robed judge. It is in this light that one must, however briefly, examine the part played in our society by the *rebel*. The Scandinavian *waldganger* of the Middle Ages hid in the forest, there to fend for himself as best he could. He did not, and could not, think of robbing the State and the laws of their sanctity. Not so our modern rebel. I should like to stress only one point; the rebel seizes reality and especially the reality that our world has become such that as Ernst Jünger put it, prejudice and passions always require their tribute of blood. He is the one who accepts, and lives, our contradictions, in a state of protest. At the same time, he becomes the symbol of acceptance and rejection. His protest can adopt the form of throwing a bomb at the Grand-Duke's carriage or of dying like Socrates. But essentially he represents what Albert Camus has called *justice* in a moral sense, that is, the certitude that, by protesting, in whatever fashion, he is right with the world as it should be. He will never consider himself as an outlaw. Neither will we, passive spectators of his creative despair, since under our masks we know that he is right. His judges condemned Socrates for his irony, which in our world is an illegitimate form of protest; in the same way do we condemn rebels for the trappings of their actions, not for their nature. They are our inner self and when we destroy them, it is like a piqued nation which turns against its gods and does away with its idols, while still believing in them. However, rebels are situated at the lowest level of protest and this is precisely why we honour them; their protest corresponds to our own level of spirituality. Socrates knew that his irony answered the moral question which was in his judges' minds and that, if he was ironic enough, the very measure of his irony would calm their consciences and that he would die. He adapted his level of spirituality to theirs. And he died, knowing what he was doing, while *they* did not know. So that his death was as ironic as his life.

But apart from criminals and rebels, there are others who refuse to accept, who challenge the established moral order. They are the ones we should be particularly interested in, since it is through their undercurrent exertions that our moral values, over the ages, are slowly transformed and adapted to new conditions of life. In some cases, their influence is self-evident: Rousseau, for example, who created a new concept of social order and family relationships, or Freud, who destroyed some fundamental misconceptions with regard to human behaviour. But these are, I should think, shock-examples. What I should like to deal with at greater length is what could be called the subterraneous transmission of personal moral values. And the example which I feel represents best this particular mode of transmission is that of Baudelaire.

On the surface, Baudelaire lived according to the moral values of his day and age; according, like most of us, to the precepts of the police code. That is, that he never infringed the law to the extent of being trapped and branded for his "immorality." This only means that, again like most of us, he lived on the moral fringe. Who indeed, if the moral code were fully respected, is not a criminal? To all outward appearances, therefore, Baudelaire, in spite of what was considered by his milieu and family as "artistic idiosyncracies" can be said to be quite representative of the attitude of most men of letters of his time in the conduct of his life.

But ironically *Les Fleurs du mal* was condemned by a court of law precisely for its immorality. However, this condemnation was considered as a necessary fact of creative literary life and Flaubert was branded in the same manner. It served, and Baudelaire protested vehemently against this condemnation, to emphasize the poet's strict adherence to the moral principles of his time. Also, it was part of the "moral system" that a provocative writer should be the object of official disapproval. The society in which Baudelaire lived (that of the Second French Empire) was notorious for its lack of morals; Baudelaire, in essence, was not condemned because his poems smacked of immorality, although that was the official reason given at the trial, so much as because he had created a new poetical form had introduced in literature what Victor Hugo called a "new shiver"; society in fact, condemned the shiver and the expression of it, not the absence of morality which it thought lay behind a new poetical flowering. The judgment was on poetry and Baudelaire's morals were condemned only by extension, by refraction.

Superficially, he lived according to the rules of the times. But he believed in another set of rules, which were entirely spiritual; and it is this set of rules which Baudelaire has bequeathed us. The point I want to stress is not Baudelaire's spirituality; in a world of spirituality, he might have devised a materialistic way of thinking. The important fact is that he lived his inner life *against* the general grain of the society around him. In our society, personal moral values are creative only when they are lived as a form of protest and it is even to be wondered whether they are not that protest itself. This is true, at least in the case of Baudelaire. What he did was to define the environment in which moral values can best thrive. He began by re-creating a relationship between man and God. Indeed, when one considers his historical context, he created a god and the attitude man should have toward him. An attitude of despair and love; he believed that the unfathomable difference between God and the human creature was necessary to man; that the particular kind of despair which is born from the realization of this difference is the highest form of love which man can bestow upon his God. By so doing, he resolved one important contradiction which is at the basis of man's relation to God; servitude is Love. At the same time that he accepted the Deity, Baudelaire rejected humanity as it was, as it still is. "Cattle," he said, and by turning his back upon his fellow-beings, strengthened the binding union between himself and God.

By refining man's sensibility while at the same time replacing this sensibility in its right historical eternal context, Baudelaire accelerated the process of disintegration of moral values as he knew them; that is, he confronted man with an image of himself which forced him to take a position of truth with regard to himself in relation to God and the world. All moral values which put a stop to this confrontation are nefarious. Such are the sublime moral values; from one century to the other, they remain the same. Courage, honour, the sense of duty: these are moral values which do not change, which society as a whole refuses to see changed; they represent that immobile stability which humanity needs not to progress. We cling to them, they are safe, they give us instinctively a sense of security. And for that very reason, although they are values, they are amoral, like stones. They are the result of man's atavistic refusal of change. Whereas sin and remorse, love and hatred, the sense of beauty and ugliness oblige man to affirm his identity in a personal manner. Alone do we sin, love and admire, each in his own acceptance or rejection. Without this singular affirmation, no moral progress is possible.

With this in mind, Baudelaire can be understood as the very type of man who resumes in himself one global aspect of humanity and who is able to express a moral desire in terms which humanity can eventually understand and accept. These men are few; they are prophets in the sense that, lost among us, they are inwardly forced to project outside of themselves an atom of undiscovered, or unexploited truth in man. In an indefinable way, they make humanity progress, against its own grain. But it is too late; humanity has already absorbed their message before it is aware that it has changed. Fortunately, for it would appear that humanity will always refuse to change of its own accord.

What is revealing in this interactive process is that society, in the end, irretrievably accepts only those moral values, or values of sensibility, against which it has most strongly reacted. Indeed, if one wanted to be scientific, one could say that humanity's protests in this domain are a barometer of truth. In the interchange between creative man and mankind, mankind's protest takes a form of untruth, which is necessary if the transmission of values is to be achieved. Humanity conceives the creative man only as a being of protest; it views him, and can view him only, as a rebel of the primary kind, one who does not exist outside the shock values of his protest. In a sense it is right, since there is an element of primary protest in Baudelaire; this element exists in order to blind humanity. Baudelaire's supposed immorality, for example, is this element of semi-truth. He appeared to his times, and still very often appears to us, as a being of protest, when in fact he is a being of unification. The inner direction of his thought was not toward liberty, but toward spiritual unity. What humanity, which is essentially a being of multiplicity, searches for is liberty, not inwardness. But, in its own intuitive fashion, it felt that Baudelaire's apparent forms of protest were not directed against its craving for liberty; however, it could sense in him only the superficial mode of protest. In a negative way, society understood Baudelaire, but it could destroy only one part of him. And it is in the strength of this destruction that one finds the truth and magnitude of Baudelaire's inner development. André Gide wrote that there existed a sort of complicity between the great man and his times. It does exist, but it is often a negative complicity. This negativeness breeds an intensification of conscience in the great man and an upward movement toward the Personal. And the result in time of this transcendence is that Baudelaire's sensibility is transformed into an ethic, which, in the spiritual context, can only be the first step toward mystical flowering.

I have suggested that it is only through a particular kind of great man, a man whose sensibility and intuition at least equal his intelligence, that moral values are transferred from one generation to the other. This transfer is difficult to perceive; one can discuss it afterwards. But is it possible to study its mechanism? It all happens as if the universe were subconsciously ready to receive a certain message at a given time. We express this when we say that an idea is "in the air." Could it not be that humanity reacts as a whole, as it were, cyclically, but at the same time according to laws which cannot be defined beforehand, only afterwards perceived?

However that may be, it appears to be essential that this subconcious message which comes from humanity itself should be expressed in the singular; that is, that one man should find in the depths of himself that truth which humanity craves for, cannot express and in spite of itself in an agony of refusal seizes upon, as soon as it has been enunciated. That man is the great man. In our civilization, he is the prophet and, even if his language is clear and understandable, he is surrounded by secrecy and mystery. He needs to be in order to maintain that kind of intellectual and spiritual elevation without which his words will be of no avail. Mankind is unable to believe the truth unless it is shrouded. The ways of truth are not straightforward; neither is its enunciator. He is a creature apart and the distance between himself and those for whom his message is meant must be as wide as the sea. Values of truth, moral values are travellers of darkness.

Our century has changed all this. It has done away with secrecy and has not replaced it by light. Let us take the example of Einstein. Here is a man of truth, who saw the universe as it is, transformed it and, having done so, despaired. This cosmic despair was the part of truth which he was meant to pass on to humanity. This message has not been passed on. Why?

What we are now witnessing is a very peculiar phenomenon. There is no doubt that our part of humanity is afraid, to such an extent that it is prepared to go to any length to forget this fear. It has invented an immense realm of "forgetting" pleasures and has submitted to them. We believe that we can spend our lives in such a variety of pleasures that it will be impossible for us to take stock. In the seventeenth century, Pascal wrote that all the ills of mankind came from the simple fact that man found it impossible to remain alone in a room. There, one presumes, he could think about his past, his present and his future; we find this even more impossible today, and those who would not find it impossible are considered as erratic and unsociable.

In short, we live in an escapist society. But there is the "great man" with, embedded in himself, a grain of truth. He is still among us, a living contradiction to all we breathe for. Energetically, our society has set about destroying him. The process has been simple enough; we have transformed the great man into a star. We have vulgarized him; and Einstein's despair in front of the universe has been reduced, through constant depreciating repetition, to proportions impossible to understand. This old man is filled with terror at the sight of a moral value gone mad; is the world consequently to be destroyed? Is man, at one stroke, to disavow his whole past? The problem of peace in our time has transcended usual political reasoning; it has become the single moral problem worth reflecting upon. It is a problem of such frightening magnitude that, in order to preserve not only its sanity (without acting upon it) but also in order to go on as if nothing had happened (which is what it really wants), Society, finding it beyond its means to destroy the idea, set out to destroy the man. Not that Einstein ever became a figure of fun or of scandal; this would have been the easy, but also temporary way out. Machiavelism won the day and Einstein became a "personality," a figure which is halfway between the eccentric and the outright crank. This process of transformation and debasement is subtle and, if one considers the mechanical order involved, quite exciting. His views were given the widest possible diffusion; but they were simplified to the point of vulgarity. And especially, they were shorn of their main moral component: the personal involvement of the man who uttered the prophecy. Einstein was showered with public recognition; he figured in glossy magazines and newspapers alongside film stars and popular writers. He was made one of them. And his pronouncements on the future of Humanity became like those of Marilyn Monroe on Man. It is the old Communist tactic of the amalgam, but reduced to the point of absurdity. The "great man" was unmade. He was brought down to the stature of the common man; he became a prophet whose mantle has been stolen. How can truth reach and discomfort us, when it is similar to the absurd? "Of course, there will be an end to all that; the world is bound to perish," thought we; "but why should Einstein say it, and what is the value of years of thought if that be the result?" Of the inner torments of the man, of his sense of guilt and responsibility, the very moral core of his conclusion (presented to the world as if it were a working formula), we heard nothing.

The plight of Einstein is further intensified in the case of Oppenheimer, the modern apocalyptic figure. Let us remember that when the first atom bomb exploded, somewhere in barren America, Oppenheimer witnessed the event. The eruption of scientific madness transformed him into an analogical prophet. While the contraption went off, he stood there and recited Hindu mystical poetry, thus uniting two contradictory worlds. He is our Nero, hailing the destruction of Rome with song and harp. While Einstein, a man of strength and purity, could not become what he was meant to become, Oppenheimer, abandoning those features of his being which at Los Alamos, transformed him for a few instants into a prophetic link, rejected his robes and stood, or tried to stand, in society as one of us. But the dictatorship of the mass is satisfied only with total annihilation; Oppenheimer was condemned and destroyed, willingly. He entered the superficial spirit of history and agreed that it should kill him. There is nothing so ridiculous as the prophet in the dance-hall and Oppenheimer accepted this fate.

Contrary to Einstein, he condoned the rules of our game of destruction of the supreme individual, and gave in to the pressures of the mass. Oppenheimer's downwards odyssey brings us one stage further in the process of disintegration which we are witnessing; challenging by mass inertia, he willingly accepted its "superiority," in exactly the same sense that the victims of the Moscow trials accepted disappearance inside Stalin's monolithic dream. In a sense, Oppenheimer's action enhanced (albeit in a negative fashion) his position as a prophetic symbol. But this is to make virtue of annihilation.

Undoubtedly, all generations have tried to run away from the moral responsibility which was being thrust upon them by individuals with a moral sensibility. But we are the first generation which has been able to transform any concept into cheap non-existence. Therefore, we are the first generation with a global responsibility in this regard. And apparently, we have chosen to use all the means of influence at our command, not to intensify the strength of moral thinking, but to debase it. It is an aspect of the triumph of mass-communications which bodes ill for the future of the Western world. I have the impression that the Communist world is, superficially at least, better equipped to meet the challenge created by the transmission of moral values. Perhaps not because it is less corrupt than our own; this is a debatable question; but because in its own sanctimonious way, it underlines constantly some primary idealistic values of mankind. At the same time, because its values are primary in nature, it leaves a greater scope for the penetration of those "deleterious" values of sensibility which transform and enhance one's conception of moral values. To a certain extent, Communism finds itself in the same position as the world in which Baudelaire lived; the same values are triumphant in both societies.

In his book, *Incognito*, Petru Dumitriu dealt with the inner transformation of that society. "Some men," he says, "will suddenly stand up in the wilderness of conformity, speaking an uncomprehensible language which will reach a few souls. By their presence, by their inner vitality, and although, to all outward appearances, they will conform, these exceptional human beings will transform the world in which they live, fertilizing placidity with doubt." This process is possible in a society the aim of which is not to debase men, however much it debases him in fact, whereas it is rendered impossible in ours, whose aim appears systematically to reduce man to the lowest common denominator. It is in that sense that the Communist world can be conceived as superior to ours. Man there is not replete with distracting and debilitating moral titillations; he has yet to learn how to run away from fatality; he has yet to accept the supremacy of diversion. This is our state of being, our decadence and our doom.

Paradoxically, this process of disintegration might be our salvation because it might also mean the disappearance, in the long run, of the supremacy of the mass in moral matters. While all values are being destroyed, a new man might be born. It is an anarchistic principle, but Humanity as a whole seems to advance toward disappearance and rebirth. For example, Reformation was built, theologically, on this principle. But it liberated man at a time of particular historical stress; it put him on the way toward finding the principles of his own moral behaviour, but without having been able beforehand to strengthen the individual. Now we are living in a world where the true individual has to be strengthened, if only to survive. Any thinking man today is forced, by the nature of the mass pressures which are exercised upon him, to live against society. By inner necessity, all men who detach themselves from the beliefs of the mass are anti-social. In a Kierkegaardian sense they are "a-teleological."

To a certain extent, the mystic is similar to the rebel; but, whereas the rebel rejects the world as it is, the mystic accepts it *as it should be*. That is, he projects himself into that world of the future we are instinctively craving for, of which we feel we are dispossessed. Mystical purification is an intellectual process as much as a spiritual one and it is as an intellectual ascesis that it is interesting to us now; although the intellectual-spiritual imbrication is such that we cannot entirely separate one from the other, yet the emphasis might be put on one of the two components. With this distinction in mind, it becomes evident that intellectual mysticism, that is, the process of self-unification through thought, is more easily attainable, and that therefore it can propagate itself more freely. It is the intellectual mystic which is the man of the future, because he accepts and transcends the world at the same time. The rebel is witness to the strength of the spirit, but his negative attitude toward the world corrupts his message; he is still a by-product of this world he condemns, exactly as the anti-capitalist world which Fourier dreamt of was a by-product of capitalism. Intellectual mysticism is the contrary of nihilism. Its main aim (and it is by this trait that we recognize the intellectual mystic) is not negatively to reject, but to look for that part of truth which is to be found at the bottom of all "untruth" or "exaggeration." I believe for example, that it is essential not to decry our machine-civilization so much as to try and extract the *positive* meaning of the techniques of material sciences. Our machine-civilization is carried forward by a superior determinism and, again, I believe that it is among the ranks of the scientists, scientifically intuitive, that the intellectual mystics will be found, once these scientists have abandoned material theoretizing to bring their minds to bear on the problems of the spirit. It is they who might someday transform moral values into values of destiny.

Moral values, as we conceive and live them today, are an end in themselves. Therefore, we have corrupted the very meaning of morality; and when our society debases men who consider moral values as a phenomenon of evolution, adaptable to man's needs, it is acting perfectly normally. One cannot but be distressed; but distressed, not because this debasement is happening, but because there is cause for it to happen. Therein lies the drama. It is because moral values have been transformed from a means to an end that they are so easily, and necessarily, perverted. Their very existence as values is perverted; they are not what they are, or seem to be. As soon as one stresses the cosmic necessity of moral values, one realizes that the debasement of values we are witnessing today is a normal degenerative process and that decadence should set in. Ionesco writes: "Take a circle, caress it and it becomes vicious." This is what we are doing with moral values; we have caressed them, in the sense that we have elevated them to the stature of ideals. But moral values are not an Ideal Being; they seek revenge in their deformity. The man of the future, that is, one who refuses to endorse this false transmutation of moral values, finds it impossible to abide by these mass-laws, because he instinctively senses that these mass-laws are in the process of becoming a thing of the past. As far as he is concerned, they are already a thing of the past; he views the debilitating process with a certain degree of equanimity. He alone, in the midst of the great catastrophe which surrounds us and which is engulfing moral values as they are conceived and practised now, will remain protected. Noah's Ark was but a symbol of the salvation of the few. Noah goes out and selects the best of the animal kingdom; they are protected while water submerges the land of the Old. So will it be with those who have put knowledge above moral values. The present evolution of moral values tends toward the breaking-up of man; he is morally and voluntarily corseted and seeking for breath. He will eventually break up and there will remain only the few who have reached truth across the desert of moral conformity.

In the "Grand Inquisitor," Dostoevski does not try to define truth. Even though Dostoevski's method is artistic rather than philosophical, nevertheless, it remains as a solid image. The Grand Inquisitor seeks to define truth; he cannot because Christ, who is a repository of truth, remains silent. The Inquisitor questions him, prods, is left to deal with the subject himself. Finally, it is through his own contradictions that he arrives at a measure of definition. Truth gushes out, but in a negative fashion, as against the Inquisitor's argumentation. Real truth is still to be found only in Christ's silence. It is the same with our moral values. We are destroying them, by debilitating the only message which could give them a lease on life; the moral conception of men who do not believe in them as we do. In fact, we are hoarding them, as does the miser who hides his poor treasure, buries it in the ground and when the flood comes, finds his acre of wealth carried away. And it is swept away, because it is in the nature of a superior determinism that it should thus have disappeared. By stultifying our moral values, we are hastening the process of disappearance. These are our inquisitorial contradictions.

Meanwhile the intellectual values of the future, irrevocably, are coming into being. They are stronger for all the agitation which surrounds them. But if man is ever to accede to another level, another dimension, which is that, not of morals, but of knowledge, of Mind, of the Spirit, the destruction of static moral values has to be accomplished. This destruction cannot but be in the making, and a new Noah, somewhere, is already building his transcendental Ark.

SELECTED BIBLIOGRAPHY

For a more comprehensive bibliography of the literature prior to October 1958, we recommend E. Albert and C. Kluckhohn (eds.), *A Selected Bibliography on Values, Ethics and Esthetics in the Behavioural Sciences and Philosophy*, Glencoe, Ill., The Free Press, 1959.

Paperback editions are shown in brackets.

General

Allport, G., and P. Vernon, *A Study of Values*, Boston, Houghton Mifflin, 1931
Benedict, K., *Race, Science and Politics*, N.Y., Viking (Compass), 1962
Boulding, K., *The Image: Knowledge in Life and Society*, Ann Arbor, University of Michigan Press, 1961
Drucker, P., *The New Society*, N.Y., Harper, 1949
Frye, H., *By Liberal Things*, Toronto, Clarke Irwin, 1959
Haskins, C., *Of Societies and Men*, N.Y., Viking (Compass), 1960
Hocking, W., *Man and the State*, New Haven, Yale University Press, 1926
Hook, S., *Determinism and Freedom in the Age of Modern Science*, N.Y., Collier Books, 1961
Howells, W., *Mankind in the Making*, Garden City, N.Y., Doubleday, 1959
Huxley, A., *Brave New World Revisited*, London, Chatto & Windus, 1959
Jackson, B. (Ward), *Faith and Freedom*, London, Hamish Hamilton, 1954
Jaspers, K., *The Future of Mankind*, Chicago, University of Chicago Press, 1961
Kluckhohn, C., *The Scientific Study of Values*, Toronto, University of Toronto Press, (University of Toronto Installation Lectures), 1959
——— "Shifts in American Values," in E. Morison (ed.), *The American Style*, N.Y., Harper, 1958
Koestler, A., *The Yogi and The Commissar and Other Essays*, London, Cape, 1945
Lasswell, H., *Power and Personality*, N.Y., Viking (Compass), 1962
Mumford, L., *The Story of Utopias*, N.Y., Viking (Compass), 1962
Northropt, F., *Philosophical Anthropology and Practical Policies*, N.Y., Macmillan, 1960
*Naegele, Kaspar, *From De Tocqueville to Myrdal: A Research Memorandum on Selected Studies in American Values*, Harvard Values Study, Cambridge, Mass., 1949
Orwell, G., *Animal Farm*, London, Penguin, 1951
Paton, H., *The Modern Predicament*, N.Y., Macmillan (Collier Books), 1963
Piddington, R., *Limits of Mankind*, Bristol, J. Wright, 1956
Simmel, G., *Conflict*, Glencoe, Ill., The Free Press, 1955

---
*Conference participant.

Sorokin, P., *Crisis of Our Age*, N.Y., Dutton, 1942
Toynbee, A., *A Study of History*, vol. VIII, London, Oxford University Press, 1961
────── *Civilization on Trial*, N.Y., Oxford University Press, 1948
Weiner, N., *The Human Use of Human Beings*, Boston, Houghton Mifflin, 1950

Social

Aubert, V., "Competition and Dissensus: Two Types of Conflict and of Conflict Resolution," *Journal of Conflict Resolution*, VII. 1 (1963): 26–42.
Carstairs, G., *This Island Now*, The Reith Lectures, 1962
Case, C., *Essays in Social Values*, Los Angeles, University of Southern California Press, 1944
Cohn, W., "Social Status and the Ambivalence Hypothesis: Some Critical Notes and a Suggestion," *American Sociological Review*, 25.4 (1960): 508–13.
Flüegal, J., *Man, Morals and Society*, Middlesex, Eng., Pelican, 1955
Gurin, G., et al., *Americans View Their Mental Health*, N.Y., Basic Books, 1960
Hamlin, D., (ed.), *The Price of Being Canadian*, Toronto, University of Toronto Press, 1961
Hughes, E., "Dilemmas and Contradictions of Status," in *Men and Their Work*, Glencoe, Ill., Free Press, 1958
Jackson, E., "Status Consistency and Symptoms of Stress," *American Sociological Review*, 27.4 (1962), 469–80
Kardiner, A., *The Psychological Frontiers of Society*, N.Y., Columbia University Press, 1945
────── *Sex and Morality*, N.Y., Bobbs-Merrill, 1954
Lederer, W., and E. Burdick, *The Ugly American*, London, V. Gollancz, 1959
Lewis, O., *The Children of Sanchez*, London, Secker & Warburg, 1962
*Macdonald, R. St. J. (ed.), *Current Law and Social Problems*, 2 vols., Toronto, University of Toronto Press, 1960
Madigan, F., "Role Satisfaction and Length of Life in a Closed Population," *American Journal of Sociology*, 67.6 (1962): 640–9
Malinowski, B., *Freedom and Civilization*, N.Y., Roy Publishers, 1944
Maritain, J., *Reflections on America*, N.Y., Scribner, 1958
Martineau, H., *Society in America*, Garden City, N.Y., Doubleday (Anchor), 1961
Mayo, E., *The Human Problems of an Industrial Civilization*, N.Y., Viking (Compass), 1960
Merton, R., *Contemporary Social Problems*, N.Y., Harcourt Brace, 1961
Mills, C., *The Power Elite*, N.Y., Oxford University Press, 1956
────── *White Collar*, N.Y., Oxford University Press, 1951
Molnar, T., *Decline of the Intellectual*, N.Y., World Publishing Co. (Meridian), 1961
Morroe, B. et al., *Freedom and Control in Modern Society*, N.Y., Nostrand, 1954
*Naegele, Kaspar, et al. (ed.), *Canadian Society*, Toronto, Macmillan, 1961
────── (jt. ed.), *Theories of Society*, 2 vols., Glencoe, Ill., The Free Press, 1959
Packard, V., *The Status Seekers*, N.Y., McKay (Cardinal), 1961
Parsons, T., *The Social System*, Glencoe, Ill., Free Press, 1951
Rose, A. (ed.), *The Institution of Advanced Societies*, Minneapolis, Minnesota Press, 1958
Rosenberg, S. (ed.), *A Humane Society*, Toronto, University of Toronto Press, 1962
Russell, B., *Human Society in Ethics and Politics*, N.Y., Simon & Schuster, 1955
Santayana, G., *Character and Opinion in the United States*, N.Y., Scribner, 1956
Sapir, E., "Culture: Genuine and Spurious," in D. Mandelbaum (ed.), *Selected Writings of Edward Sapir*, Berkeley, University of California Press, 1951

──────────
*Conference participant.

Shapiro, H. (ed.), *Man, Culture and Society*, N.Y., Oxford University Press, 1956
Sorokin, P., *Man and Society in Calamity*, N.Y., Dutton, 1942
Tannenbaum, F., *Slave and Citizen: The Negro in the Americas*, N.Y., Random House (Vintage), 1963
Tiryakian, E. (ed.), *Sociological Theory, Values and Sociological Change: Essays in Honour of P. A. Sorokin*, N.Y., Free Press, 1963
Warner, W., *American Life, Dream and Reality*, Chicago, University of Chicago Press (Phoenix), 1962
Whyte, W., *The Organization Man*, Garden City, N.Y., Doubleday (Anchor), 1957
Williams, R., *American Society: A Sociological Interpretation*, N.Y., Knopf, 1958

Philosophy and Religion

Allport, G., *The Individual and His Religion*, N.Y., Macmillan, 1950
Barth, K., *Community, State and Church*, N.Y., Doubleday (Anchor)
*Baum, Gregory, *Progress and Perspectives*, N.Y., Sheed & Ward, 1962
Bennett, J., *Christian Ethics and Social Policy*, N.Y., Scribner, 1956
Brinton, C., *A History of Western Morals*, N.Y., Harcourt Brace, 1959
Ginsberg, M., "The Function of Reason in Morals," *Proceedings of the Aristotelian Society*, 39 (1938-9): 249-70
Hodger, H., *Christianity and the Modern World*, London, S.C.M. Press (Seraph), 1962
James, W., *Varieties of Religious Experience*, London, Collins (Fontana), 1960
Johnson, F., *Patterns of Ethics in America Today*, N.Y., Collier Books, 1962
Leake, C. and P. Romanell, *Can We Agree? A Scientist and a Philosopher Argue about Ethics*, Austin, University of Texas Press, 1950
Lippman, W., *The Public Philosophy*, N.Y., New American Library (Mentor), 1956
Maritain, J., *Christianity and Democracy*, N.Y., Scribner, 1944
Neibuhr, R., *Faith and History*, N.Y., Scribner, 1949
Patka, F. (ed.), *Existentialist Thinkers and Thoughts*, N.Y., Citadel Press, 1962
Russell, B., *Philosophy and Politics*, Cambridge, Cambridge University Press, 1957
*Vivas, Eliseo, *The Moral and the Ethical Life*, Chicago, Henry Regenery (Gateway), 1963
―――― "The Moral Philosophy of Corporate Man," review of E. Jordan's *The Good Life*, Chicago, University of Chicago Press, 1949; in *Ethics* (April 1950), 188-97
―――― *Creation and Discovery*, N.Y., Noonday Press, 1955

Personal

Arnorno, T. et al., *The Authoritarian Personality*, N.Y., Harper, 1950
Barrett, W., *The Irrational Man*, N.Y., Doubleday (Anchor), 1962
Bettelheim, B., *The Informed Heart*, N.Y., Macmillan, 1960
*Boucher, Jean, "The True Friends of the Lonely Crowd," *Saskatchewan Council of Public Affairs*, Regina, 1962
Freud, S., *Civilization and its Discontents*, London, Hogarth, 1939
Fromm, E., *The Sane Society*, N.Y., Rinehart, 1955
Golfman, E., *The Presentation of Self in Everyday Life*, Garden City, N.Y., Doubleday, 1959
Hook, S., "Moral Freedom in a Determined World: Responsibility and Sentimentalism," *Commentary*, 25 (1958): 431-43
James, W., *Essays on Faith and Morals*, N.Y., World Publishing Co. (Meridian), 1962

*Conference participant.

Jung, C., *The Undiscovered Self*, Boston, Little Brown, 1958
Kardiner, A., *The Individual and His Society*, N.Y., Columbia University Press, 1939
——— and L. Ovesey, *The Mark of Oppression*, N.Y., World Publishing Co. (Meridian), 1962
Kerr, W., *The Decline of Pleasure*, N.Y., Simon & Schuster, 1962
Kluckhohn, C. et al., *Personality in Nature, Society and Culture*, N.Y., Knopf, 1953
MacIver, R., *The Pursuit of Happiness*, N.Y., Simon & Schuster, 1955
Maritain, J., *The Person and the Common Good*, N.Y., Scribner
Maurois, A., *The Art of Living*, London, The Bodley Head, 1959
Menninger, K., *Man Against Himself*, N.Y., Harcourt, 1938
Mumford, L., *The Transformation of Man*, N.Y., Collier Books, 1962
Newcomb, T. (jt. ed.), *Readings in Social Psychology*, N.Y., Holt, 1947 (especially F. Allport on "Conforming Behaviour")
Niebuhr, R., *Moral Man and Immoral Society*, N.Y., Scribner, 1934
——— *The Nature and Destiny of Man*, N.Y., Scribner, 1941
Riesman, D., *Selected Essays from Individualism Reconsidered*, Glencoe, Ill., The Free Press, 1954
Russell, B., *Authority and the Individual*, N.Y., Simon & Shuster, 1949
*Underhill, Frank, "John Stuart Mill," in *Architects of Modern Thought*, Toronto, Canadian Broadcasting Corporation, 1962

Science

Bain, R., "The Scientist and His Values," *Social Forces*, 31 (1952): 106–9
Barber, B., *Science and the Social Order*, N.Y., Collier Books, 1962
Bronowski, J., *Science and Human Values*, N.Y., J. Messner, 1958
Brown, H., *The Challenge of Man's Future*, N.Y., Viking (Compass), 1956
*Cohen, I. Bernard, *Science, Servant of Man*, Boston, Little Brown, 1948
Conant, J., *Modern Science and Modern Man*, N.Y., Doubleday (Anchor), 1953
Frank, P., *Modern Science and its Philosophy*, N.Y., Collier Books, 1961
Goldston, I. (ed.), *Society and Medicine*, N.Y., International University Press, 1955
Hall, E., *Modern Science and Human Values*, Princeton, Van Nostrand, 1956
Heisenburg, W. et al., *On Modern Physics: A Non-Technical Survey of the Implications of Modern Science in all Fields of Knowledge*, N.Y., C. N. Potter, 1961
Huxley, J., *Evolutionary Ethics*, London, Pilot, 1947
Lovell, B., *The Individual and the Universe* (B.B.C. Reith Lectures, 1958), Oxford University Press (Galaxy)
Munitz, M., *Space, Time and Creation: Philosophical Aspects of Scientific Cosmology*, N.Y., Collier Books, 1961
Northropt, F., *The Logic of Sciences and the Humanities*, N.Y., Macmillan, 1947
Obler, C. and H. Estrin, *The New Scientist*, N.Y., Doubleday (Anchor), 1962
Pollard, W., *Physicist and Christian*, N.Y., Seabury, 1961
Polyani, M., *Science, Faith and Society*, London, Oxford University Press, 1946
Snow, C., *Two Cultures and the Scientific Revolution*, N.Y., Cambridge University Press, 1959
Szent-Györgyl, A., "Science, Ethics and Politics," *Science 125*, 1957
*Vivas, Eliseo, "Science and Studies of Man," in *Scientism and Values*, Princeton, Princeton University Press, 1961
Wigner, E. (ed.), *Physical Science and Human Values*, Princeton, Princeton University Press, 1947

———

*Conference participant.

Politics

Acton, Lord, *Essays on Freedom and Power*, Cleveland, World Publishing Co. (Meridian), 1962
Adler, M., *The Idea of Freedom*, Garden City, N.Y., Doubleday, 1958
Arendt, H., *The Origins of Totalitarianism*, N.Y., Harcourt Brace, 1951
Barker, E., *Reflections on Government*, N.Y., Oxford University Press, 1958
Bell, D., *The End of Ideology: On the Exhaustion of Political Ideas in the Fifties*, N.Y., Collier Books, 1963
Burns, E., *Ideas in Conflict: The Political Theories of the Contemporary World*, N.Y., Norton, 1960
Carritt, E., *Morals and Politics*, Oxford, Clarendon Press, 1958
Croce, B., *Politics and Morals*, N.Y., Philosophical Library, 1945
Forcey, C., *The Crossroads of Liberalism*, N.Y., Oxford University Press, 1961
Friedrich, C. (ed.), *Authority*, Cambridge, Mass., Harvard University Press, 1958
Goldson, J. (ed.), *Outer Space in World Politics*, N.Y., Frederick Praeger, 1963
Hallowell, J., *The Moral Foundation of Democracy*, Chicago, University of Chicago Press, 1954
Hook, S., *Political Power and Personal Freedom: Critical Studies in Democracy, Communism and Civil Rights*, N.Y., Collier Books, 1962
*Jouvenel, Bertrand de, *On Power: Its Nature and the History of its Growth*, N.Y., Viking, 1949
────── *Sovereignty: An Inquiry into the Political Good*, Chicago, University of Chicago Press (Phoenix), 1957
────── *The Pure Theory of Politics*, Cambridge, Cambridge University Press, 1963 (bibliography)
Kornhauser, W., *The Politics of Mass Society*, Glencoe, Ill., Free Press, 1959
Lane, R., *Political Life: Why People Get Involved in Politics*, Glencoe, Ill., Free Press, 1959 (bibliography)
Laski, H., *The American Democracy: A Commentary and an Interpretation*, N.Y., Viking, 1948
Lasswell, H. and A. Kaplan, *Power and Society: A Framework for Political Inquiry*, New Haven, Yale University Press, 1950
MacPherson, C., *The Political Theory of Possessive Individualism*, Oxford, Clarendon Press, 1962
Maritain, J., *Man and the State*, Chicago, University of Chicago Press (Phoenix), 1951
Mills, C., *Power, Politics and People*, N.Y., Oxford University Press, 1963
Mitchell, W., "The Ambivalent Social Status of the American Politician," *Western Political Quarterly*, 12 (1959), 683–9
Morre, W., "But Some Are More Equal Than Others," *American Sociological Review*, 28.1 (1963): 13–18, 26–8
Polanyi, C., *The Logic of Liberty*, Chicago, University of Chicago Press, 1951
Popper, K., *The Open Society and its Enemies*, 2nd ed., London, Routledge, 1952
*Sartori, Giovanni, *Democratic Theory*, Detroit, Wayne State University Press, 1963 (bibliography)
Schumpeter, J., *Capitalism, Socialism and Democracy*, N.Y., Harper (Torchbooks), 1962
Scott, F., *Civil Liberties and Canadian Federalism*, Toronto, University of Toronto Press, 1959
Tocqueville, A. de, *Democracy in America*, N.Y., Oxford University Press, 1947
Tussman, J., *Obligation and the Body Politic*, N.Y., Oxford University Press, 1960
*Underhill, Frank, *In Search of Canadian Liberalism*, Toronto, Macmillan, 1960

───────
*Conference participant.

———— *The Image of Canada*, Saint John, N.B., University of New Brunswick, 1962
Watson, G. (ed.), *The Unservile State: Essays in Liberty and Welfare*, London, Macmillan, 1957
Weldon, T., *States and Morals*, N.Y., McGraw-Hill, 1947

Economics

*Balogh, Thomas, *Unequal Partners*, 2 vols., Oxford, Blackwell, 1963
Berle, A., *The American Economic Republic*, N.Y., Harcourt Brace, 1963
Boulding, K., *The Organizational Revolution*, N.Y., Harper, 1953
Bronfenbrenner, M., "Two Concepts of Economic Freedom," *Ethics 65*, 1955
Childs, M. and D. Cater, *Ethics in a Business Society*, N.Y., Harper, 1958
Clark, J., *Alternative to Serfdom*, N.Y., Knopf, 1948
Cropsey, J., "What is Welfare Economics?" *Ethics 65*, 1955
Dahl, R. and C. Lindblom, *Politics, Economics and Welfare*, N.Y., Harper, 1953
Drucker, P., *The Practice of Management*, N.Y., Harper, 1954
———— *The End of Economic Man*, N.Y., John Day, 1939
Finer, H., *Road to Reaction*, Boston, Little Brown, 1945
Friedman, J., "Study and Practice of Planning," in *International Social Science Journal* (UNESCO), XI, no. 3 (1959)
Galbraith, J., *The Affluent Society*, Boston, Houghton Mifflin, 1958
Hayek, F., *The Road to Serfdom*, Chicago, University of Chicago Press (Phoenix), 1944
Innis, H., "Industrialism and Cultural Values," in *The Bias of Communication*, Toronto, University of Toronto Press, 1951
Keynes, J., *Essays in Biography*, N.Y., Harcourt, 1933
Lerner, A., *The Economics of Control*, N.Y., Macmillan, 1944
Little, A., *A Critique of Welfare Economics*, Oxford, Oxford University Press, 1960 (biblography)
Mises, L. von, *The Anti-Capitalistic Mentality*, Princeton, Van Nostrand, 1950
Myint, H., *Theories of Welfare Economics*, London, Longmans, 1948
Myrdal, G., *Beyond the Welfare State*, New Haven, Yale University Press, 1960
Pigou, A., *The Economics of Welfare*, 4th ed., London, Macmillan, 1932
Randall, C., *A Creed for Free Enterprise*, Boston, Little Brown, 1952
Reid, T. (ed.), *Economic Planning in a Democratic Society?* Toronto, University of Toronto Press, 1963 (bibliography)
Sutton, F. et al., *The American Business Creed*, Cambridge, Mass., Harvard University Press, 1956
Tawney, R., *Equality*, 4th ed., London, Allen & Unwin, 1952
Taylor, O., *Economics and Liberalism*, Cambridge, Mass., Harvard University Press, 1955
Underhill, Frank et al., *Social Planning for Canada*, Toronto, Thomas Nelson, 1935
Veblen, T., *The Theory of the Leisure Class*, N.Y., Viking (Mentor), 1953
Wallich, H., *The Cost of Freedom: Conservatives and Modern Capitalism*, N.Y., Collier Books, 1962
Ward, D. (ed.), *Goals of Economic Life*, N.Y., Harper, 1953 (especially F. Knight, "Conflict of Values: Freedom and Justice")
Wootton, B., *Freedom under Planning*, London, Allen & Unwin, 1946
Wyllie, I., *The Self-Made Man in America*, New Brunswick, Rutgers University Press, 1954

*Conference participant.

BOARD OF DIRECTORS

CANADIAN INSTITUTE ON PUBLIC AFFAIRS

President: Dr. Norman A. M. MacKenzie
Vice-Presidents: Mr. Alastair W. Gillespie
　　　　　　　　 The Hon. J. Keiller Mackay
　　　　　　　　 Mr. Harry Wolfson
Treasurer: Mr. Francis K. Eady

MRS. DORIS ANDERSON, Editor, *Chatelaine*
MR. DEREK BEDSON, Clerk of the Executive Council, Province of Manitoba
M. PIERRE DE BELLEFEUILLE, Rédacteur, *Le Magazine Maclean*
M. JEAN BOUCHER, Directeur, Direction de la Citoyenneté, Ministère de la Citoyenneté et de l'Immigration, Ottawa
MR. DUNCAN F. CAMERON, Consultant in Museum Planning and Development
MR. WILLIAM R. CARROLL, Director, Canada Packers Limited
DR. W. T. EASTERBROOK, Chairman, Department of Political Economy, University of Toronto
MR. ARNOLD EDINBOROUGH, President and Editor, Saturday Night Publications Limited
MR. D. M. GRAHAM, Director of Education, Forest Hill Village, Toronto
DR. WILLIAM M. KILBOURN, Chairman, Humanities Division, York University
DR. ROBERT M. MACINTOSH, Assistant General Manager, Bank of Nova Scotia
MISS CHRISTINA MCDOUGALL, Program Organizer, Public Affairs Department, Canadian Broadcasting Corporation
PROF. JOHN S. MORGAN, School of Social Work, University of Toronto
MR. NEIL MORRISON, Joint Secretary, Royal Commission on Bilingualism and Biculturalism
MR. LEWIS PERINBAM, Secretary, Canadian National Commission for UNESCO
THE REV. J. A. RAFTIS, Institute of Mediaeval Studies, University of Toronto
MR. RONALD S. RITCHIE, Director, Imperial Oil Limited
MISS MARION V. ROYCE, Director, Women's Bureau, Department of Labour, Ottawa
MR. JULIAN L. SMITH, Manager, Retail Division, United Co-operatives of Ontario
MRS. RYRIE SMITH, Past President, National Council, Young Women's Christian Association
MRS. A. K. STUART, Executive Member, Women's Committee, Toronto Art Gallery
MR. BERNARD TROTTER, General Supervisor, Public Affairs, Canadian Broadcasting Corporation
MR. JOHN WHITEHOUSE, Education and Research Director, Textile Workers Union of America

Executive Secretary: Mr. Timothy E. H. Reid

C.I.P.A. PUBLICATIONS

The following publications are available from the University of Toronto Press:

Economic Planning in a Democratic Society? ed. T. E. H. Reid. Based on the 9th Winter Conference, 1963. Pp. viii, 86, $1.75.
    Articles by: Harry Johnson, Jacques Parizeau, Arthur Shenfield, James Tobin, R. V. Yohe, George F. Bain, Thorbjörn Carlsson, Clarence Barber, Scott Gordon, H. I. Macdonald, Robert MacIntosh, Carl Pollock, Larry Sefton, Arthur Smith, Eric Trigg.

The New Europe, ed. D. L. B. Hamlin. Based on the 31st Couchiching Conference, 1962. Pp. xii, 108, $2.00.
    Articles by: Raymond Aron, John Holmes, William Clark, William Diebold Jr., Shaun Herron, C. R. Ford, Eric Pettersson, A. W. Gillespie, Vladimir Velebit, Rudolf Meimberg, Charles Caccia, Peter Munk, Henry Mhun, Peyton Lyon, Jan Tupker, Harry Wolfson.

The Press and the Public, ed. D. L. B. Hamlin. Based on the 8th Winter Conference, 1962, Pp. x, 38, $1.50.
    Articles by: Louis M. Lyons, Stuart Keate, Robert Fulford.

Diplomacy in Evolution, ed. D. L. B. Hamlin. Based on the 30th Couchiching Conference, 1961, Pp. viii, 128, $2.00.
    Articles by: Ritchie Calder, Gordon Coburn, André Philip, H. R. Vohra, Harry Wolfson, John Holmes, Henry Kissinger, Geoffrey Bourne, G. R. Davy, Gordon Hawkins, C. B. Marshall, John Polanyi, James Eayrs, Duff Roblin.

The Price of Being Canadian, ed. D. L. B. Hamlin. Based on the 7th Winter Conference, 1961. Pp. x, 54, $1.50.
    Articles by: Douglas V. LePan, Hugh MacLennan, Frank Underhill, André Raynauld.

The following publications are available from the Canadian Institute on Public Affairs, 244 St. George St., Toronto, Ont.:

Is Business Reshaping Society?, ed. D. L. B. Hamlin. Based on the 6th Winter Conference, 1960. Pp. viii, 56, $1.00.
    Articles by: Earle MacPhee, W. H. Evans, Maurice Lamontagne, Pierre Berton, Ian McRae, W. P. Scott, W. E. Williams, A. W. Gillespie, J. R. M. Wilson, Herbert Lank, Stanley Knowles, B. S. Keirstead, Adolf Berle Jr., T. W. Kent, Monteath Douglas.

Crisis: '58, ed. Catherine D. McLean. Based on the 27th Couchiching Conference, 1958. Pp. iv, 100, $1.00.

Articles by: Lester Pearson, Fritz Erler, Robert Bowie, Thomas A. Mann, Ellis A. Johnson, Robert McKenzie, Chan Htoon, Eugene Forsey, A. D. Misener, Gerald Graham.

www.ingramcontent.com/pod-product-compliance
Lightning Source LLC
Chambersburg PA
CBHW020257030426
42336CB00010B/816